# COOKED

## *An Inner City Nursing Memoir*

Carol Karels

Published by
Arcania Press
65 Zabriskie Street
Hackensack, NJ 07601

All inquiries to:
info@arcaniapress.com

Cover Design
Barry Scheinkopf

Book Design
Robert Gerber

ISBN: 0-9767714-0-3 (paperback)

Printed in the United States of America

Dedicated to Mom

# Acknowledgements

My nursing stories were written twenty years after the events occurred. Names, situations and stories I had long forgotten mysteriously surfaced in a most vivid manner during the writing process, similar to the slow release of a genie in a bottle. I thank all my friends, relatives and historic preservation colleagues who encouraged me to write these stories, especially when we learned the nursing school had closed and that Cook County Hospital might be demolished and the stories forgotten.

Thanks to Mom for getting me into the nursing profession in a roundabout way and thanks to Dad for paving the path for my subsequent writing career, in an even more roundabout way.

Thanks to fellow County grads, especially Genelle Bajoras Cadenas (Class of '72) and Elsie Hernandez Flores (Class of '74), who validated my memories and reminded me of more. Thanks to all CCSN alumni who have kept the alumni association going.

Thanks to Barry Scheinkopf of The Writing Center in Englewood Cliffs, NJ, for critiquing a chapter a week, as the memories came back to me, and for designing the cover. Thanks to my Leonia, New Jersey friends--nurses and non-nurses--who edited the book, hosted book parties, read the book in its various phases and gave valuable feedback, and lent their design expertise. Special thanks go to Ena Scrivani, Leslie Ayvazian, Pam Fenwick and

Melinda Aranda.

Thanks to Jane Stern, the author of "Ambulance Girl" for her positive encouragement and suggestions.

Thanks to the Midwest Center for Nursing History, for rescuing what they could after Cook County School of Nursing closed, including class photos and old uniforms. Thanks to all nurses who worked at Cook County Hospital and knew the true secret of the place--that despite its reputation, there was no more fulfilling place to practice our profession. Our time there made us better nurses and better people. Working at 'the County' made us appreciate what's really worthwhile in life and dismiss what's not.

Thanks to the voters of Cook County for building a magnificent new public hospital in 2001 where all can go to get treated with dignity. Thanks to the members of Preservation Chicago for their efforts to preserve Cook County Hospital as a landmark.

Thanks to my historic preservation colleague Kevin Tremble for the title suggestion and for his valuable advice at all stages of preparation. Thanks to Robert Gerber, Ron Anzalone and Alex McCausland for being perfectionists at what they do--producing books. Thanks to all my relatives, including the Morey's and Kathy Cartwright, for helping me when I most needed it.

Thanks to the nurses at Northwest Continuum in Longview, Washington for the excellent care they gave my mother in the last years of her life.

Thanks to those who choose to enter the nursing profession knowing it is no bed of roses, but that the rewards are immense. I thank all my patients for helping me learn life's lessons. Finally, thanks to my daughter Beth for providing me with the gift of motherhood.

# Introduction

*"If all the tales are told, retell them, Brother.*
*If few attend, let those who listen feel."*

In May 1971, I was accepted into Cook County School of Nursing, affiliated with Chicago's Cook County Hospital. That same month, *LOOK* Magazine featured an article entitled *Cook County Hospital: The Terrible Place.* This was the first paragraph of the story:

"Cook County Hospital, with 2,000 beds, is one of the largest public charity hospitals in the country. Its new director frankly describes it as a 'sea of mediocrity' with a few 'islands of excellence.' Its angry interns call it a '19th-century sick house.' It is a terrible place."

The article later goes on to describe how fly swatters were routinely used in the eighteen operating rooms, for the hospital lacked air conditioning on all but the most critical floors--the burn unit and the intensive care units. It was a hospital filled with block-long wards, with only curtains separating the beds. Twenty to sixty patients shared one bathroom. Wheelchairs were wooden and beds were hand cranked. It was a hospital without call lights--if patients needed a nurse, they yelled for one. Patients were often sent to X-ray naked because clean gowns and sheets were unavailable. Lab specimens took days to get results. Nurses often purchased toilet paper and other necessities with their own money. Finding electrical outlets that would accept three-pronged plugs, for EKG machines and emergency carts, was next to impossible. On obstetrical floors, vaginal exams were routinely done in full view of other patients.

Fortunately I didn't see that article until 2005, for if I had, I might never have undertaken the exciting and memorable journey to become a nurse at Cook County Hospital.

What I *did* know when I applied was that Chicago had been providing some type of health care for the poor ever since 1835. First there was the Public Almshouse, then the Poor Farm, and for children, the Orphan Asylum. To handle the medical needs of the growing indigent population, Cook County Hospital was built in 1913, a gorgeous Beaux Arts building with a terra cotta facade, unusual for a public hospital. By the time it was complete, it had a total bed capacity of 3,400!

Throughout most of the twentieth century, the hospital, known as 'the County,' was a medical refuge for the inner city poor who filled its beds. Every week, hundreds of patients turned away from other hospitals because of race or poverty sought and received medical care at the County, travelling, on average, eight miles. They brought their breakfast, lunch and dinner, for all knew the wait would be long, but that they'd eventually get the medical care they needed.

Providing high-quality nursing care was also a top priority. At a time when there were only 550 trained nurses in the nation, the Illinois Training School for Nurses opened in 1880. When it closed in 1929, Cook County School of Nursing was started, modeled after Florence Nightingale's training schools for nurses in England. CCSN trained thousands of nurses, many of whom stayed on to work at Cook County Hospital.

Doctors from all over the world also received their training at

County. And thousands of life-saving medical procedures were developed on its massive wards.

The hospital was also world reknowned for many medical initiatives, including its Burn Unit, prenatal care, Trauma Unit and Blood Bank. In the years before Medicare, Medicaid, legalized abortions, and managed healthcare, County's idealistic nurses and doctors were among the first in the nation to go on strike for better working conditions, and the first to go to jail for their convictions.

My story takes place in the early 1970's, a bleak period when drug dealing, gang violence, tuberculosis and teen pregnancies were commonplace in the inner city. The title refers to the burnout that is common with nurses and other caregivers, especially if they are working long hours with insufficient staffing--a condition far too prevalent in hospital environments. Vacations and changes of venue helped me cope. Too many other dedicated and caring nurses simply choose to leave the profession after their initial burnout, or like me, after ten years, resulting in a nursing shortage worldwide.

*COOKED* is both my personal story and a history of inner city medicine in another time. It tells of the compassion, caregiving, dedication, chaos and risks that took place on County's huge wards and in the surrounding neighborhoods. Names have been changed. Most characters are composites. The stories come from my memories.

# ❖ 1 ❖

When I think back on the numerous assaults to my senses I experienced as a young nurse, it's ironic that only one, the birth of a baby, ever made me faint. It was a sweltering Friday morning at Chicago's Cook County Hospital, the largest public hospital in the U.S. I was a first-year nursing student at Cook County School of Nursing, one of the most prestigious Florence Nightingale-style training schools in the country. Or so I had been told. As part of our 'Introduction to Nursing' class, we had to observe a routine delivery. Little did I know that, at Cook County Hospital, few deliveries were routine.

I overslept that morning, skipped breakfast, and ran through the musty tunnel that connected the nursing school to the hospital to catch up with my classmates. Outside it was already 97 degrees. In the tunnel, one lined with leaky steam pipes and old mattresses, it was easily 100. Sweat dripped from the elevator operator's forehead as he pressed the button for the fifth floor. "We're cookin' today," he said, as he mopped his brow.

The Woman's Ward was an oven. My classmates and I were herded to the dressing room to don the required pink scrub outfits. Once dressed, our instructor escorted us to the labor line—two rows of stretchers occupied by dozens of girls and women in various stages of labor. The sweaty women were thrashing, grunting, cursing and screaming. One pre-teen was in full leather restraints, and continually screamed, "I don't want this baby. I don't want this baby!" An older one next to her bellowed, "God in Heaven. I've had it. Tie my tubes!" One removed her gown and threw her cover sheet onto the floor, leaving her body totally exposed. I'd never seen women act that way. I'd never imagined that having a baby was like this.

Our instructor approached the head nurse and said, "My students are here to see a delivery. Can you let me know when one gets close?"

"It's going to be a good hour," the nurse replied. "The closest one is 7 centimeters, and she's been stuck there a while. Why don't you show your students the delivery rooms in the meantime?"

There were ten delivery rooms, all set up exactly the same, none air-conditioned. Each had a delivery table and an incubator. On a tray were antiseptics and various medications. And in a sterile bowl were a scissors and two clamps. Our instructor showed us the different kinds of steel forceps used in difficult deliveries, all of which looked like medieval instruments of torture.

The smell of fried bacon from the restaurant below wafted into the delivery room. I would have given anything, at that moment, for an egg and bacon sandwich on a roll. I glanced out the open window. Dozens of night shift employees were leaving the hospital, racing toward the approaching El train. The train stopped long enough to pick up and discharge passengers, then sped by the idling cars and trucks on the Eisenhower Expressway, all stuck in morning rush hour. I wondered why anyone would drive into the city during rush hour. The traffic sat there for hours every morning.

I heard the nurse yell, "Delivery coming to Room Three. I need a doctor! *Now!*"

I poked my head out of the room and was nearly run down by the transporter, who was sprinting down the hall, pushing a screaming Hispanic woman on a stretcher. I jumped back and ran to the far wall.

"Cálmate! Let's get you into this bed the right way," the nurse yelled, while the woman screamed, "Ay, Dios mío." Once the woman was on the delivery table, the nurse cut off her undergarments, revealing the baby's head!

"This baby's out!" yelled the nurse.

The woman grunted, and the bloody little body slithered out. The nurse grabbed it with her bare hands, fumbling it as if it were a football. The doctor raced in, still pulling the gloves onto his hands. Seeing that the baby was out, he clamped the umbilical cord in two places, and then severed it with a scissors. The nurse wrapped the baby in a blanket and placed it in the incubator. Then, with the exception of the screams from the labor line, there was silence.

Moments later, my instructor broke the silence. "Where did *she* come from?"

"The ER," said the nurse.

"Are they all that fast?" I asked the nurse.

The ER transporter said, "Her husband said this is her eighth kid, so she probably went into labor just before she got in her car."

The woman's blood-stained legs lay open in the stirrups. Her pelvis was completely exposed with the umbilical cord hanging out her vagina. I felt embarrassed and kept averting my eyes. The doctor sat on a stool at the end of her bed, his now gloved hands held in the air expectantly.

"What are we waiting for?" I whispered to my instructor.

"She hasn't delivered her placenta yet."

"Doesn't it usually come out right away?"

"Sometimes. Not always."

Flies buzzed around the room, entering through the open windows. They buzzed around my head, and around the woman's exposed pelvis. One landed on her large toe and sat there a minute or so. The doctor flicked it away with the back of his gloved hand.

I felt nauseous and lightheaded. The room began to spin. I took deep breaths and began rocking in place, like a nervous child who has to pee.

Then the doctor put his left hand on her still large abdomen. With his right, he tugged on the umbilical cord, which was wrapped around a clamp. The last thing I remembered, before I collapsed to the floor, was the bloody placenta slithering into the waiting steel bowl.

The last words I heard were, "Get her out of here." And the last thing I felt were strong arms pulling my limp body into the hall. When I came to, I faced two of my male classmates, also in pink, kneeling on the floor facing me. I felt like I was floating, and wanted the feeling to continue. But my fellow students lifted me to my feet and sat me in a nearby chair. My instructor felt for my pulse and asked if I was OK.

"I'm all right," I said, still dazed. "I guess I'm not used to the heat. And I didn't eat breakfast."

"And you're not used to seeing a delivery!" said my pale male classmate, who looked as if he was relieved to get out of the delivery room too.

Then my teacher scolded me. "One thing you'll learn as a County nurse is to eat before you come to the wards because once you do, there's no letup. And if you're running on empty, you're going to burn out in no time. And then what good are you? You're a neophyte now but by the time you graduate from this place, you'll be ready to work in any battlefield."

She made it sound like nursing boot camp. I wondered if my fainting spell inspired this speech, or if it was the standard one given after every group's first visit to the hospital.

# ❖ 2 ❖

A year earlier, I couldn't have imagined nursing school in my future. I'd always thought nurses knew they were going to be a nurse from a young age. I thought nursing was a calling, like the nunnery or the priesthood. Teaching, journalism and social work were all careers I'd considered but *never* nursing. I'd never been seriously ill, nor had anyone in my family. I hated shots and the sight of blood made me woozy. *All good reasons not to be a nurse,* I thought.

I'd only been inside one hospital. Actually, I'd only been inside the volunteer department of that hospital--Cook County Hospital-- on Chicago's near west side. I first visited there when I was sixteen. I was helping my mother deliver a load of donated coats, shirts, pants, and shoes. TheVolunteer Department maintained a Charity Wardrobe for patients who needed clean clothes to wear after they were discharged. Mom was the volunteer responsible for keeping it well supplied. She said patients who had been admitted in the warm months were often not discharged until the cold months. So they needed coats. Many of them had no shoes when they were admitted, or shoes that didn't fit properly or were rotting on their feet. And the clothes of many were in such bad shape they had to be incinerated.

Before we'd dropped the clothes off at the hospital, Mom told my brother John and me to look through the coats and pick one out that we fancied. That's how I got a 'new' winter coat every year. After we'd picked out our own coats, she deposited the rest at the Volunteer Department, located adjacent to the Emergency Room. She always managed to find a few doctors, orderlies and nurses to help her unload her truck. I was so impressed at the teamwork, at how everybody dropped everything to help Mom.

After unloading her truck, she introduced us to Missus Jones, the 80-year old, 88-pound volunteer who greeted Mom with a hug, and then shouted in her high-pitched voice, "Missus Karels is here. We gonna *fill* the cupboard today!"

In addition to clothes, Mom also stocked the volunteer office with donated books, magazines and snacks that could be distributed to the patients. The clothes came from churches and synagogues all over the city. The magazines and snacks came directly from the factory—Johnson Publishing for *Ebony* and *Essence* magazines, Casa Escobar for Spanish magazines, and Keebler's warehouse for cookies and crackers. Nobody turned down Mom's requests for *the County.*

The day my brother and I helped my mother, we saw a new side to her. She was more than the 'class parent' who baked cupcakes for every school party and came along on all the field trips. She knew every back street in Chicago, and told us stories about every neighborhood. She showed us where famous shootouts were, where the stockyards used to be, where Mayor Daley lived, where Tokyo Rose worked, and where Hugh Hefner kept his Playboy bunnies. The security guards at every publishing company knew her by name, and she chatted with all of them as they helped her load magazines into her truck. At the churches and synagogues where she made stops, she shared jokes with the priests and rabbis as they sorted through piles of donated coats.

Between pickups, Mom took us to lunch at Braverman's Cafeteria on the rundown west side (brisket on rye and potato pancakes) and to Batz' Restaurant on the near south side for dessert (freshly made rice pudding). We also stopped at the bagel bakery in Skokie (a few blocks from Queen of Peace Catholic Church, which donated the nicest coats). For a special treat, we'd have pastries at Lutz' Bakery on west Montrose. It was clear Mom loved and missed the excitement and diversity of the city in which she had been raised. She wanted us to see there was more to life than the fields and streams of the suburb in which we lived.

When I didn't go with her, I enjoyed the stories she told about the people she'd met that day in the nursing school and in the volunteer office. But she told me the *real* stories were *inside* the huge dilapidated hospital, behind the worn façade, the grimy windows and the walls with peeling gray paint. Inside those walls, she said, were real-life saints. These saints took care of the sickest and poorest Chicagoans. The saints, she said, were the nurses and doctors, and only they could tell the real stories about the hospital.

In all the years Mom volunteered, she never suggested I join the ranks of those 'saints.' She knew I wanted to be a teacher. But I became discouraged when my guidance counselor said there were too many teachers in Illinois, and that there might not be a job after graduation.

"Have you thought about a career in journalism?" my guidance counselor asked. I loved writing. I had written for the local newspaper since I was thirteen. I was the News Editor of my school paper. My favorite book was the biography of journalist Nelly Bly. I fantasized that my grades were good enough for Northwestern's School of Journalism and that my family could afford the tuition. But we bought our clothes at thrift shops. We didn't have a color TV. And Mom did the laundry once a week at the laundromat. In the summer she hung it out to dry on the tree branches in the back yard. I assumed she did that to save money on the dryer. I knew we weren't poor, but still, going to Northwestern was just a fantasy.

I had applied to only one university, the University of Illinois at Chicago Circle, and was accepted. I made an appointment to meet with an admissions counselor. She took me on a tour of the campus, and we passed a lunchtime anti-Vietnam protest march.

"Where are the dorms?" I asked the admissions counselor, after taking the tour.

"Circle Campus doesn't provide student housing," she told me, looking surprised that I didn't know. "This is a commuter school."

*A commuter school! How could I have not known that! I didn't want to commute to college!*

To complicate things even further, that night my father announced his intention to quit his job and start his own company. He was a sales engineer. He traveled constantly and fought with his boss incessantly. He ate Tums by the roll for his heartburn, and jogged every morning to control his elevated blood pressure. And now he was getting chest pains. He told us he'd be dead in six months if he didn't quit his job. My father and I had simultaneously reached a critical juncture in life. If he didn't quit his job, he'd be dead. If he did quit his job and started his own business, there wouldn't be *any* money for college tuition.

I discussed my dwindling options with Mom. After a few days, she suggested I apply to Cook County School of Nursing.

"I know you've never thought about nursing, but it's only $600 a year for room, board, *and* tuition. You'll be in the city. You'll have a room of your own. You can apply for the Elgin nursing scholarship. If you graduate, you'll be an RN making good money in three years. You'll be getting an education *and* an adventure."

For my family, the purpose of life was to have adventures. My father was an outings leader in the Sierra Club. Almost every weekend we canoed on midwest rivers or explored wild caves in southern

Indiana. We were often the only children around the campfire, listening to stories told by women who chained themselves to trees, men who re-enacted the journey of the Voyageurs and inner city pioneers who restored historic homes in dangerous, graffiti-filled neighborhoods.

We had visited Mexico City on the train when I was fifteen. And we had traveled all over the U.S. in a Volkswagen bus with two Old Town canoes on top. We'd already visited over 40 states. Even though my father never bought tents, we camped everywhere. We slept under canoes, under the stars in the desert and under the protective canopies of trees in the forest. We learned early on to put up with black flies, sand in our hair and food, mosquitoes, ticks, snakes, scorpions, incessant rain and headwinds on lakes, wet sneakers, wet wood that wouldn't burn, muddy clothes and dirty underwear. Yes, I knew about adventure. So in that spirit of adventure, I applied to Cook County School of Nursing, took the entrance test, had an interview, and was quickly accepted.

## ❖ 3 ❖

My neighbors were shocked that my parents would send me off to school on Chicago's dangerous west side. For the most part, they were second-generation Polish, Italian and Irish immigrants who had recently fled Chicago's neighborhoods—the 'white flighters.'

"Why are you sending your daughter to that ghetto nursing school," one asked my mother, "when she could attend Elgin Community College? The west side is full of gangs, shootings and drugs. For God's sake! She's your only daughter. She could be killed!"

Mom just smiled. She loved the place and was confident I'd grow to love it too. She knew there were police all over the place.

My high school guidance counselor said, "It's an absurd plan, Carol. You've never expressed any interest in nursing. You'll be miserable there, doing the things nursing students do."

*What about life as a nursing student?* I imagined it a somber one, like that of a nun in training. Suddenly, I couldn't imagine myself wearing an ankle length uniform with a tiny white organza cap on my head, doing the things that nursing students did. What *did* they do anyway? I wondered. I hadn't a clue.

A few weeks later the guidance officer called me back in to her office. "I checked into that school and it's a recruiting ground for minority nurses. You're wasting your potential. You'll be such an outsider."

*An outsider!* I'd felt like an outsider for years in the suburbs. To start, I was always the 'wrong' religion. My father was a lapsed Southern Baptist from Texas and my Mom a lapsed Irish Catholic from Chicago (even though she regularly lit candles at Holy Name Cathedral and made pilgrimages to the Shrine of Mary at Notre Dame de Chicago Church on Chicago's west side). Even so, my parents expected my brother and me to attend the closest church every Sunday. Since the Catholic Church was just down the block, that was the one we attended, as did most of the community.

We were the only kids who weren't baptized and who didn't attend Catechism. We were the only kids who showed up to Mass without parents. And we remained immobile while everyone else went up to receive communion.

Later, we felt like outsiders in high school. Our suburb, which developed overnight on cornfields, didn't have a high school so we were bused to the nearby town, which had two. Half of my junior high class was bused to the high school on the east side of the town, which had a large minority population. The rest of us were bused to the west side of the town, which was predominantly snobby WASPs. There, we 'immigrant Catholics' were treated like intruders, considered low-class and subtly excluded from many social events.

One town friend I'd made invited me to her home one day after school, an unusual invitation. Unexpectedly, her father was home. She introduced me to him as "My friend Carol, from Streamwood."

The father then called his daughter into the kitchen. In a voice loud enough for me to hear, he said, "Didn't I tell you I don't want those Streamwood greasers in our house?" My friend's father was the only one to express it, within my earshot, but I knew many other townie parents felt the same way. The Streamwood kids were the greasers, the children of immigrants, the Catholics. We were the ones who needed new grammar schools every three years because 'Catholics bred like rabbits.' We were the ones who made the townies' property taxes soar.

I wasn't Catholic. I wasn't a greaser. My parents weren't immigrants. And we had moved there from Iowa, not from Chicago. There were only two kids in my family. My Dad was in *Who's Who in the Midwest!* But it didn't matter. The Streamwood kids were all lumped together as undesirables. We were dumped into the town school system, against the town's wishes. Surely, inner city black kids couldn't affect me more negatively than them. So the possibility of being an 'outsider' at Cook County School of Nursing didn't bother me one bit. I looked forward to it.

I spent the summer before starting nursing school working at the local golf club. I was paid $1.25 per hour to clear tables and pour coffee. The owner also expected me to pass out towels to the women golfers in the shower, type up the lunch specials, pull the weeds in the driveway, and fill in for the lifeguard—even though I couldn't swim.

My boss, one of five Italian brothers who ran the club, rarely spoke to me except to bark orders. "Carol! Shine the mirrors! Scrub the mildew off the fixtures! Mop the floor! Cut up these lemons!" I felt like Cinderella there. His daughter was my age, a pampered teen who spent her days around the club pool, counting the days before she left for Southern Illinois University--a major party school.

In late August, the day after I'd helped make hundreds of hors d'oeuvres for a wedding banquet, he said, "You did good today, Carol. I'm raising your pay to $1.50 per hour next week."

"I won't be coming back next week," I told him. "I'm moving to the city to attend Cook County Hospital School of Nursing."

"Cook County Hospital?" he responded. "Why in the world would you want to go there?! I grew up in that neighborhood and still have family there. They tell me the place won't last another two years. It's falling apart and probably won't get accredited by the state. And if it doesn't get accredited, it will close. Did they tell you that when you applied?"

The Director didn't tell me a lot when I applied. She didn't tell me that *LOOK* Magazine had just printed a feature story entitled "Cook County Hospital: The Terrible Place." Nor did she tell me that three-year hospital-based nursing schools were being closed all over the country. Or that the Illinois Nurse's Association was encouraging future nurses to attend 4-year BSN programs. Perhaps she didn't know. Perhaps her only concern was recruiting nurses to work at Cook County Hospital. Ignorance was bliss.

First graduating class of Illinois Training School for Nurses, circa 1883.
This is how I imagined nursing students still looked and dressed.
The dress and cap hadn't changed much in the 1970's.

## ❖ 4 ❖

Mom drove me to Cook County School of Nursing on a hot, steamy August Sunday. She parked her pickup truck behind the school loading dock. The elderly security guard stood up and grinned as we approached.

"You kin leave the truck here, Missus Karels," he said. "Jest gimme the keys and I'll move it if I haf to."

"Thanks a million, Mr. Otis," she said. "This is my daughter Carol. She's starting nursing school here tomorrow."

"Well, we be so glad to have you here," he smiled, and he patted my shoulder with his long, bony black hands. Mom handed him the keys, and we each grabbed a handle on the side of the trunk and headed toward the basement elevator. When we reached the first floor, we headed toward the front desk. There, a cheerful, buxom receptionist in a navy blue suit greeted us.

"So you finally got your daughter to join us, Missus Karels?"

She winked at me and said, "We been working on her to get you here," she laughed. "You got Room 947, overlooking *downtown* Chicago. Here's your key, sugar, and enough food coupons to last you a month. Your classes start 9 a.m. *sharp* tomorrow on the second floor. And make sure you read these house rules, too," she said.

She handed me a sheet of paper. "Your momma can rest at night if you follow them."

"Thanks, Mrs. Rawlins," said Mom, and we headed toward the elevators, reading the house rules together. *No appliances. No food in the rooms. No men above the seventh floor. 8 p.m. curfew on weekdays. 10 p.m. curfew on weekends.*

"These rules sound like they haven't been updated since the school opened," I said.

The elevator stopped on the seventh floor and an impeccably dressed woman in a blue suit and white gloves came over to make sure there were no men in the elevator. When she saw there weren't, she smiled and pressed the button to send us up to the ninth floor.

My room looked like a furnished walk-in closet. A cream-colored chenille bedspread, as well as two starched white sheets, lay on the bed. The floors were waxed and shiny. Perfect for a nunnery, I thought. Mom stayed for a few minutes, then kissed me goodbye. I hadn't even unpacked when a student in an oversized T-shirt and slippers walked in and introduced herself.

"Are you Carol?" she asked. "I'm Genelle, your 'big sister.' I've been waiting for you."

I had received a letter earlier in the week informing me that I would have a 'big sister' who would familiarize me with the school. Genelle was a senior who lived three doors down. She looked like a gypsy, with dark black hair and heavily lined eyes.

"Welcome to Cook County School of Nursing," she grinned. "You're gonna love it here." She asked how much I knew about the place.

I told her I knew nothing except the Volunteer Office.

She pointed out the seven buildings that made up the hospital—three for adults, one for children, one for psychiatric patients, a clinic and the morgue. As she spoke, I heard sirens and noticed two emergency vehicles pull into an alley behind the huge main building.

"It'll take you a few sleepless nights before you get used to all the sirens here," she said. "This is the largest medical center in the world. There are six other hospitals besides this one, so you'll hear plenty of sirens the first week. After that, you won't hear them. They'll be there, but your brain tunes them out."

She told me we were fifteen blocks from downtown Chicago, ten blocks from the University of Illinois Circle Campus, six blocks from Little Italy, and four blocks from the Chicago Stadium. "I wouldn't recommend walking to any of them—night or day."

Seeing a portable fan in my room, she said, "That's a no-no. We have a wonderful maid named Sophie who cleans your room, changes your linen, and confiscates appliances. These buildings aren't wired for anything beyond the basic light switch. The hospital isn't even air-conditioned."

Based on what my guidance counselor had told me, I thought I'd be the only white student in the school. And I assumed everyone would be like me, right out of high school. Yet, all the new students on my floor were white, and most had been out of high school for a few years. I introduced myself to twenty-one year old Tammi, from Washington State; to nineteen-year old Amy, from Chinatown, to eighteen-year old Melissa, from the suburbs, to twenty-year old Lisa, from the south side of Chicago, and to 40-year old Ellen, who already had a degree and a career in another field.

Melissa had been the valedictorian of her high school class. She said she'd always wanted to be a nurse, and that Cook County School of Nursing was the ultimate challenge.

Lisa said she partied so hard in her first year of college that she flunked out. "My Mom heard this place was tough, like the Army, and made me come here to get my act together."

Amy said she was recruited for Cook County School of Nursing in her high school. She said three black girls from her class were accepted. Ellen said she wanted a more challenging and rewarding career.

Tammi told us that her mother had trained at Cook County School of Nursing years before. "I've already had two years of college," she said, "and now *I know* I want to be a nurse. My mother said this school has the highest standards in nurses training. I wonder if they still have the Victorian teas in the parlor." *Teas in the parlor?*

"Florence Nightingale started the tradition," she explained. "Before her time, nurses were prostitutes or drunk old women. When she started nurse's training schools, she changed the image of nursing. 'Taking tea,' instead of swilling ale, was part of the whole image change. And this school continued that tradition."

On the first day of school, I encountered the rest of my class. The group looked more like a gathering of anti-war activists and Black Panthers than future nurses. Lounging on the floor outside the classrooms, underneath the oil painting of Florence Nightingale, was a group of young black students laughing and talking loudly, acting as if they knew each other well.

Many sported towering afro hairdos, a symbol of the Black Pride Movement. (The few black students in my high school, none of whom were the least bit militant, still straightened their hair.) As more black students joined the group, a few exchanged black power salutes, raising their clenched right fist into the air.

A handful of Hispanic girls talked excitedly and laughed together in another corner. They too seemed to know one another. There were about a dozen men, most with long hair and moustaches or large afros, who looked more like rock musicians than future nurses. The rest were women of all ages and races standing around, wearing T-shirts and jeans, making small talk and waiting for the classroom doors to open. *Nobody in that room looked like they had a calling to be a nurse.*

The classroom doors finally opened and we all took seats. One male student, who wore a towering afro and sunglasses, found a seat in the back row. He put his feet on the chair in front of him, and started reading the sports section of the *Chicago Sun Times.* He continued reading the paper as attendance was called, and even after the director of the school began her welcoming speech.

"I welcome all of you," the frail, silver-haired director began. "This is my twenty-first year here. This school is, as you all surely know, one of the finest nursing schools in the world. As proof of the continuing prestige of this school, your class is the largest class ever with 150 students! Nearly half of you have college degrees already. And your class is only the second to have men. When I attended nursing school, nurses couldn't be married, yet a number of you are. And a number of you have children. You are the nurses of the future."

After her welcome speech, she divided us into four groups for a building tour. First, we visited the library, adjacent to our classrooms. It had crystal chandeliers, antique desks with brass lamps, and mahogany bookcases filled with leather-bound books.

From there, we proceeded to 'The Blue Room,' an elaborately furnished Victorian parlor filled with antiques and two grand pianos.

"This is where you can entertain guests of the opposite sex," our guide told us, "and where our social events, *including our teas,* are held."

Next, we were taken down to the tunnel. "This tunnel will take you to any building in the complex," said our guide.

We spent the next ten minutes traversing the smelly, gray tunnel, the walls of which were lined with broken stretchers, wheelchairs, linen carts and old mattresses. Every once in a while a hot puff of steam escaped from the numerous pipes on the ceiling.

Finally, we emerged back at the nursing school. "You won't be going to the hospital for several months," she said, "but when you do, always use the tunnel, day or night, winter or summer."

After lunch, we were introduced to the teachers who would instruct us in Microbiology, Chemistry, Anatomy and Physiology, and the History of Nursing. We learned that Malcolm X College would give us college credits for our science courses.

Mr. Pritiboy and Miss Thorny, the Chemistry teachers, greeted us with cigarettes dangling from their mouths. Mr. Prausnitz, the Anatomy teacher, was a sad-looking, emaciated man in his sixties, with a thick German accent. He wore a suit far too big for his bony frame. Mr. McNamara, who would teach us Math and History of Nursing, sported a three-piece suit and a handle-bar moustache. He shared with the class that he was single and that he and his male lover were trying to adopt a baby.

Later, three old Polish women measured us for our uniforms and aprons. With pins in their mouths, they expertly ran their hands up and down our bodies and wrote down our measurements. Each had her white hair pinned in a bun, and wore a neatly pressed and starched gray uniform, and white hose and shoes. I couldn't believe they hand-sewed all our uniforms, yet I noticed several bolts of blue and white cloth in the corner.

"We call you when everything is ready," said one, in heavily accented English. "You get six of each. When they dirty, you tie them up in a ball and take them to the laundry over there," she continued, pointing to a cage across the hall. "We wash and iron everything for you."

While getting measured, I chatted with some of the other students. As the director mentioned, several already had degrees in other fields. And many lived outside the nurse's residence.

One guy had been an Army medic and now wanted to be an ER nurse. The one with the sunglasses and big afro said he had been shot in the leg and treated in County's Trauma Unit. So he wanted to be a trauma nurse. They all had interesting and valid reasons for wanting to be nurses. *I felt like an imposter.*

I noticed that many of the younger black students already knew one another, and hung out together and acted indifferent to the rest of the class. Later in the evening, Genelle told me why.

"They know each other because a lot of them spent the summer together here," she said. "For the past two years, the school has been trying to recruit more minority students. Those who couldn't pass the entrance exam spent the summer here getting intense tutoring. They retook the test last week and half of them didn't pass. Those who did pass are angry because they thought their friends would get a second chance. But they didn't. This place is no bed of roses, even for kids who come well prepared. You'll see soon enough."

Cook County School of Nursing and Nurse's Residence

# ❖ 5 ❖

After a few weeks, I wasn't sure I'd last very long at Cook County School of Nursing either. I hadn't met any good friends yet, and I found the teachers were eccentric at best. Mr. Pritiboy and Miss Thorny both smoked during lectures and labs. Mr. Pritiboy was openly dating a senior student and always had his arm around her at school social functions. Mr. McNamara flaunted his relationship with a young black orderly with whom he always ate lunch in the cafeteria. Miss Thorny flirted with more than one girl in my class.

I had serious reservations about some of my classmates as well. One was expelled within three weeks for starting fires in the laundry room. Another was a pathological liar. One girl bragged about how she had already slept with two men from the sixth floor--a Pakistani pharmacist and a lab tech who was known for hitting on new students.

Half my class lived off-campus. The other half went home on weekends. A few of the Hispanic girls invited me to a fraternity party on nearby Ashland Avenue one Friday night. When I met them, they were dressed for some serious partying. I was in my standard jeans and peasant blouse. The frat house smelled like stale beer and marijuana. The rock music blasted so loud, I couldn't hear a word anybody said. Most of the medical students were drunk or high. They lounged on old, pumpkin-colored velvet couches and black vinyl beanbag chairs, groping whoever walked by. Although my classmates were having a ball, nothing about the scene appealed to me. When they invited me again the following week, I declined.

Tammi and Lisa immediately befriended male student nurses who lived on the sixth floor and spent most of their free time with them. In the past, the nurse's residence had provided rooms for women only, but with the gradual influx of male nurses, the rule had been changed to allow male nurses and other male professionals to live on the sixth floor of the building. They paid $40 per month rent, as did the RNs who lived on the upper floors of the fifteen-story building.

Although men weren't allowed to go past the sixth floor on the elevator, they often visited girlfriends via the staircase. The doors from the stairwell were supposed to be locked at all times, but waiting women let them in. If a man was caught above the sixth floor, he could be evicted. Miss Shimmer, the House Matron, made routine rounds on the floors in the evening, to make sure men weren't where they shouldn't be. For this reason, visiting men never hung out in the hallways, but they were often behind closed doors.

I ate most of my meals with Amy, the girl from Chinatown. Because her English was limited, she spent twice as much time on her homework as I did, regularly staying up past midnight. Although on the surface she seemed a dedicated student, she confided to me that she didn't really want to be a nurse. She wanted to get married and have children. But the man she loved was engaged to her older sister.

"He loves me, not my sister," she lamented. "But it would bring shame on my house if he married me. In the Chinese culture, the older sister must marry first."

She enrolled in nursing school, she explained, to get out of her family's apartment in Chinatown, where she had to deal with that painful reality every day.

I told her I was there more for the adventure than the nursing, and that I didn't know how much longer I'd be there either. Then we were told about "the disaster drill." Our teachers told us that health officials from the state would be monitoring the hospital's disaster-readiness and we students would be the mock disaster victims.

On the day of 'the disaster' we were all herded into the main parking lot, where dozens of makeup artists waited.

The 'disaster' was a plane crash. We spent the entire morning getting professionally made up. My makeup artist gave me an open fracture of my right thigh and a subdural hematoma.

"The bone sticking out of your leg is a dead giveaway that you need immediate help," she said. "But let's see if the doctors find the purple makeup behind your right ear. You're supposed to be unconscious, so don't answer any questions until the drill is over."

We were all on the ground, cracking jokes about our injuries and our grotesque bloody makeup, when a loud siren went off. Within minutes, staff from the hospital came running toward the parking lot and we were soon surrounded by nurses and doctors, all doing 'triage,' trying to ascertain which disaster victims needed the most help. Some of my classmates were pronounced dead and they were covered in blankets and the drill was over quickly for them. Others, whose 'injuries' seemed minor, were tagged and left behind. And those lucky ones with serious injuries, like me, were given top priority and whisked off on stretchers to the Emergency Room.

It was my first time in the hospital. Green walls and green scrub suits surrounded me. I was taken first to the Emergency Room, then to the Orthopedic Operating Room, and finally, to the Neurosurgery Ward. The doctors wrote everything they 'did' for me on a sheet of paper, which would later be evaluated by the state disaster staff. I observed my surroundings with fascination the entire time. Even though we were in the middle of a disaster drill, there were real disasters taking place all around me. At least they looked like real disasters to me. Yelling patients. Nurses running around. Beeping machines. *I was finally inside Cook County Hospital!*

Four hours after being placed on a stretcher in the parking lot, I was discharged. The doctors gave me a copy of my triage sheet, and a souvenir mask and operating room cap. When I returned to the nurse's residence, I compared notes with other classmates. Most of the students I spoke with said it was a boring exercise, a waste of time. I found the whole drill fascinating and fun. I looked forward to getting back in the hospital.

## ❖ 6 ❖

Amy dropped out of school at the end of October. She later wrote and told me she had eloped with her sister's fiancée and had moved to Canada. Both had been disowned. She was the first to leave.

After her departure, I began spending my free time with Karen, Rosie and Anne, all second-year students who lived in the rooms adjacent to mine. The group often invited me to eat dinner with them. They all had part-time jobs as student assistants on the wards, to make extra money and to get additional experience. When they spoke of their experiences, it was in a language I did not understand. They might as well have been speaking another language.

"What a madhouse last night!" one would start, during dinner. "We admitted this guy with a CVA and a sky-high BP, so the doctor injected IV Hyperstat, but he injected it too fast, and then his pressure bottomed out and we had to call a code. And of course, there was no crash cart to be found in the building. To make things worse, the transporter brought up a GI bleeder from Ward 35 who pulled out his NG tube, and there were coffee grounds all over his sheets. And then another guy, an OD, pulled out his foley when he came to, and we had to apply full leathers on him. Not to mention the woman with the suspected MI; she started getting dyspneic and tachycardic, and nobody could find a working outlet to plug in the the EKG machine. The med student must have stuck her ten times to get a blood gas." *I had no idea what they were talking about!*

One Sunday afternoon, they invited me to The Greeks restaurant for dinner. It was a long, low building directly across the street from the main entrance of Cook County Hospital. Behind it lay a grassy field, a heliport, and the ever-busy Eisenhower Expressway. It was one of the few buildings in the medical center not connected by the tunnel. Outside the restaurant, I noticed several men in green scrub suits sitting in back, laughing and sharing cigarettes.

"Those are our infamous transporters," Anne noted. "You can never find them when you need them because they're always hanging out here, or in the tunnel, smoking pot."

Inside the restaurant, I noticed a balding cashier behind the news counter. He clenched an unlit but well-chewed cigar in his mouth. A line of people waited to pay for coffee, cigarettes, chips, newspapers and greeting cards. Fans whirred overhead.

We passed a cafeteria with steam tables. A big blackboard listed the specials of the day: Fried Chicken, Baked Pork Chops, Macaroni and Cheese. The Vegetable of the Day was Collard Greens. Several uniformed hospital workers waited in line with their trays.

"We'll eat in the back," said Rosie, "in the Monkey Room."

We then passed through a narrow doorway into a bar with black booths, red carpeting, and a few scattered tables. I noticed a mural on the wall depicting a jungle scene. A few doctors in white coats sat around drinking, occasionally interrupting their conversations to watch a football play on the television above the bar.

"Ali! Another Michelob over here," gestured one doctor to a hovering Pakistani waiter.

"Make that two," said another.

"Yes, boss," said the smiling Ali, who wore a red vest and bow tie and sported a neat moustache.

A balding, swarthy, middle-aged man with bulging eyes manned the bar. Like the cashier up front, the top three buttons of his shirt were undone, revealing a mass of gray chest hair. He held a phone in his hand.

"Hey doc," he yelled, pointing to a dark-haired, unshaven doctor in scrub pants. "They need you up in the OR. Margaret says they have a bleeder so pay up and get over there." The doctor ran out of the bar, after throwing some crumpled bills onto the table.

As soon as we ordered, my new friends began talking about their recent experiences on the wards. By the time our food came, I wasn't sure I had an appetite. Although I didn't understand most of what they said, the little I did made me queasy. At first I interrupted, asking a ton of questions. Later, I just listened.

"You know, Carol, you're making us feel like old nurses," said Karen, "yet just a year ago, we didn't know any of these words either. It's hard to believe what a year in nursing school does to you." It was after five when we left The Greeks so they suggested we cut through the Emergency Room to avoid walking outside.

"Can we do that?" I asked, thinking we must surely be considered intruders. "Of course, we can," said Karen. "We're students here. The security guards just wave us through. They're here to keep out the bums, the angry boyfriends, and the gangs. Not us!"

Just inside the main entrance, hundreds of visitors were sitting on wooden benches. A huge sign read, "Emergency Room Waiting Room."

"Who are all the old women wearing white uniforms?" I asked, noticing several on a bench. They looked too old to be nurses.

"They're called 'nurses of the church,'" Karen explained. "They're like missionaries, visiting all the sick. County is *the* place to visit on Sundays. Everybody knows someone who's sick at the County. It's like a pilgrimage."

We then hurried through the Emergency Room, past rows of patients on stretchers or in wheelchairs waiting to be examined or transported elsewhere.

Seeing my wide eyes and the serious look on my face, Anne asked, "Is this your first time in the hospital, Carol?" I told her that, with the exception of the disaster drill, it was my first time inside *any* hospital. But I was looking forward to seeing more of the place.

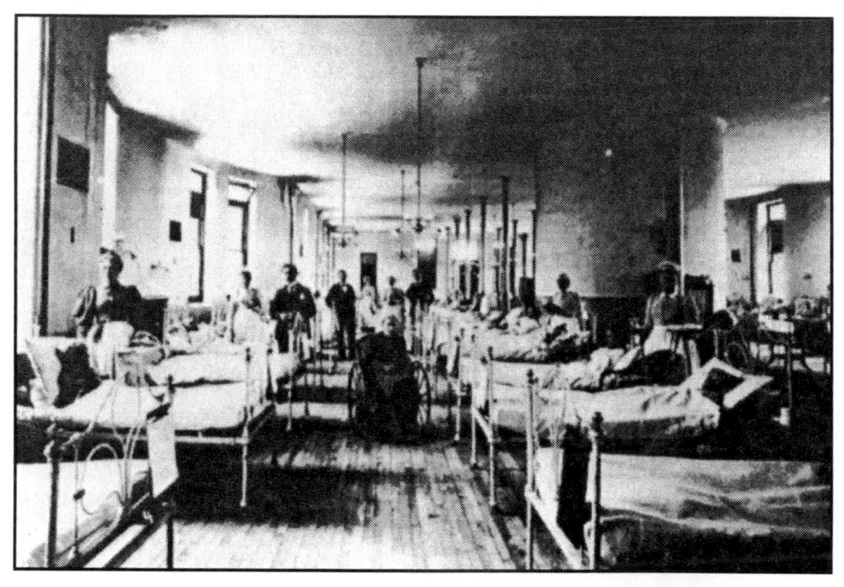

Ward 24 in the early part of the twentieth century. The ward didn't look much different in the 1970's. Only the uniforms had changed.

## ❖ 7 ❖

In November, I applied for a job as a student clerk, just to get more exposure to the hospital. The job was three evenings a week and paid $3.50 per hour.

"Report to Ward 45 on Thursday evening," said the short, bewhiskered woman in the musty basement employment office, after taking my photo for an ID. She was wearing a dark brown polyester pantsuit, men's shoes, a man's leather watch, and a short cropped afro.

The following Thursday, immediately after my last class, I raced upstairs and put on my newly purchased pink pinafore, white blouse, white stockings, and white shoes. I ran up the four flights of dingy stairs in the A Building.

There, in the clerk's office, I found a bow-legged, ebony old woman with a wide, flat nose, wearing a matted wig. I had caught her rubbing her feet, feet clad in nylons that reached up to a roll just below the knee. Her old-lady shoes rested on the floor next to her chair. Immediately she stood up, greeting me with a toothy smile.

"Hello, sugar," she smiled. "I'm Mrs. Anderson. They told me you was comin' and I be *so* glad for young blood. Too much work here for an old lady. Phone calls, charts, new admissions. And I can tell my pressure's high tonight."

She took my hand, punched my time card, and led me out of the clerk's office onto the ward. "This here's the men's side," she explained, pointing to a corridor lined with beds, most filled with older Black men.

"We got twenty mens when we full, and we *always* full. The other end is for the women—twenty of them, too. You and me gotta take care of all the paperwork for both ends. You just watch me tonight, till you get good at this. Before you know it, you'll be part of the family up here."

During the course of the evening, she taught me her job in a roundabout way. If the doctors wrote orders, she called around the hospital to make sure everything was taken care of.

"Too many things to remember," she told me. "These doctors *love* to write orders." Then she'd get on the phone.

"Pharmacy? This is Velma on Ward 45. Oh, hello Dorothy! I sure didn't recognize your voice. How you doin'?...Well, the reason I called is we're clear out of Dilantin up here. You know, them seizure pills. How soon do you think you can get some up here? A couple of hours? The nurse ain't gonna like that answer, but I'll just tell her you're backed up down there."

She took a long swig from her coffee mug, then got back on the phone with the dietary department.

"Georgine? It's Velma on Ward 45. Yes, they got me workin' up here now. 'Bout three months now. Uh huh, I *do* miss it down there, but they be nice to me up here. The reason I called is I got a couple of diet changes. Mr. Robinson in Bed Three gets a soft diet now, and Mrs. Washington in Bed Eleven needs low salt."

She took another swig from the coffee cup. She then pushed her wig back off her forehead, revealing short, nappy gray hair, and began scratching her head.

Seeing my surprised look, she laughed and said, "My granddaughters wear them afros, and keep tellin' me to get rid of this wig.

Them afros are too much work. All they do all day is pick at their hair. I like my wig. Don't even have to comb it."

A young doctor walked into the office and threw a chart on the desk. "Mr. Jackson's going home tomorrow," he said. "See if you can get his discharge meds sent up so he doesn't have to wait at the pharmacy tomorrow."

"Oh, lordy," sighed Mrs. Anderson, "that man ain't got no clothes to go home in, if he even has a home."

Once again she picked up the phone. "Archie? It's Velma. I got another man goin' home tomorrow. He'll be needin' a full set of clothes. What you say? I don't know what size, sugar, but he's a big man, 'bout 200 pounds. I reckon about six feet tall."

She covered the phone with her hand and leaned over toward me. "Go run and ask the man in Bed Six what size clothes he wears. And ask about his shoe size, too." While she spoke, a patient knocked on the window of our office, frantically pointing toward the back of the ward.

"While you're at it," she said, "see what this man wants. The nurse just left for dinner."

I stepped out of the office and the patient told me someone was vomiting in the back. Paralyzed with fear, I ran to the end of the ward to find the other nurse.

"Someone's vomiting on the other end," I told the young Filipino nurse, who was busy preparing evening medications.

"Just give heem the emesis basin," she said, not even looking up from her medication tray. *Emesis basin.*

I ran back, frantically looked through the man's nightstand, and finally handed him a steel, kidney-bean shaped bowl to vomit in. He looked at me like I was crazy, as most of the vomit already lay in a pool beside the bed. Flustered, I returned to the office and told Mrs. Anderson there was vomit all over the floor.

"Don't worry yourself 'bout that," she said. "I'll just call Housekeeping, but don't forget to ask Bed Six what size clothes he wears."

"Right," I responded, having already forgotten. I ran out to get that information. At the same moment, a frantic-looking intern popped his head in the office and dropped four tubes of blood on the desk.

"These are Mr. Jefferson's, the guy with renal failure," he said. "I checked the tests I want on the slips, but I don't have time to fill in all the information. Can you do that? I gotta get back to Ward 35. They just called me for another admission, my eighth today. Don't forget to mark STAT on them."

"These new doctors," chuckled Mrs. Anderson, "marking everything STAT like they in some private hospital. They should know by now that nothing be done STAT at the County. The lab closes at nine, and they still be doing tests from last week. If he wants the results this week, he better take 'em to the lab hisself, and do 'em hisself."

Hektoen Lab, the central lab facility, was a block away, she told me, as she reached for the phone again. Mrs. Anderson seemed to spend an inordinate amount of time on the telephone, requesting the services of transporters, housekeepers, and lab technicians, or just trying to get through to busy departments.

"I swear they know I'm calling and just don't pick up the phone," she muttered.

The other nurse returned from dinner, and asked if the Dilantin seizure medication had arrived. "No," said Mrs. Anderson, "I called that in about an hour ago. They said it would be ready in two hours. At nine, I'll send somebody down to pharmacy to get it."

The nurse protested. "I was supposed to give it at four and it's already eight!"

Looking at me, the nurse asked, "Can you run downstairs to

Ward 35 and ask Mrs. Sanchez for 300 mg. of Dilantin."

"Could you write that down?" I asked, knowing I'd never remember the drug or the name of the nurse. Looking exasperated, the nurse wrote the information down.

I raced down the staircase. Ward 35 looked *nothing* like Ward 45. Patients were lined up in the hallway on both stretchers *and* in wheelchairs. Dozens of doctors and nurses raced around the noisy floor. Many sat around a center table, conferring and writing notes.

I found Mrs. Sanchez, got the desired medication, and raced back up the stairs. The waiting nurse snatched the medication out of my hand. No smile. No thanks.

"What do they do down there?" I asked Mrs. Anderson. "It's so busy."

"That's the admitting floor, where they bring 'em up right from the Emergency Room. The busiest place in the hospital, if you ask me," she added. "I used to work down there, but they moved me up here when my (blood) pressure started gettin' high."

My thoughts came back to Ward 45 as I noticed many patients getting ready for bed. A young woman had begun to comb and braid the hair of an elderly woman, and a middle-aged patient gently spoon-fed Jell-o into the mouth of a gray-haired woman in a wheelchair. Others quietly read the Bible in their beds.

"The patients really look after each other, don't they?" I commented to Mrs. Anderson.

"Sure do," she nodded. "Nurses don't have time for all the little things, so everybody helps out. I had my babies here. And I was once a patient downstairs, on the cardiac unit. The doctors and nurses treated me real good. I tell all my friends, 'If you ever sick, come to the County.'"

"But you can go to any hospital, can't you?" I asked. "Don't you have medical insurance?"

"I got insurance, all right," she said. "And so do my family, and most of my friends. But it ain't that easy for us to go to another hospital, if you know what I mean. They always seem to be full when we're sick. The County always has a bed for us, and you be treated right here, like family."

Mrs. Anderson didn't come out and say it, but she was implying that black people couldn't get admitted to private hospitals. I found that hard to believe. It was the 1970's, not the fifties! But she had assured me that it was the case, even in 1971.

## ❖ 8 ❖

When I returned to Ward 45 a few evenings later, Mrs. Anderson greeted me with open arms and her toothy smile. "I'm so glad you back! I was afraid I scared you off." On the contrary, I couldn't wait to get back.

We had been working for about an hour when the building supervisor called. He told Mrs. Anderson he needed her to work on Ward 35 that evening because one of the clerks there called in sick. She shrugged and said, "That place is too busy. You gonna have to come with me and give me help. You're my little white shadow." She grabbed both our time cards, and unquestioning, I followed her down the flight of stairs.

Mrs. Anderson led me into Ward 35's clerk's office, which had a table, three chairs, and three telephones. Clerks were sitting in two of the three chairs. A small transistor radio played Sly and the Family Stone's latest hit. Mrs. Anderson introduced me to Miss Graham and Mr. Abdul, with whom she had worked before. Miss Graham, a curt young woman with a short, tight afro hairdo and round, wire-rimmed glasses, acknowledged our presence with a disinterested nod. Mr. Abdul was dressed like an African tribal king, wearing a brightly colored daishiki and an African hat. Garish gold rings adorned his fingers, and gold chains hung round his neck. He too, seemed to care less that we had come to help.

Mrs. Anderson found a chair for me. "Sit," she said. And I sat. "First of all," she began, "forget everything I teached you upstairs, because this here's the admitting floor. Here, you got to fill out a chart for each patient, and write their name, birthday, hospital number and doctor's name on each of these sheets of paper. Then you fill out the ID band."

"After you finish preparin' the chart," she continued, "you got to put the ID band on the patient and then put all his valuables in this here envelope. You got to write down everything they have, like 'two earrings,' 'one ring with red stone,' 'one watch with brown band,' 'fifty-two dollars,' 'one pair of slippers.' Then he has to sign. Otherwise, when it's time to go home, they be saying they had a million dollars and two diamond rings, and somebody done stole 'em."

"Then you check his clothes," she continued. "Sometimes, they come up from the ER already in a gown, with their clothes in a bag. If not, you have to wait till the nurse helps them undress, then you got to write down every piece of clothing. Even if the clothes is already in a bag, you got to take 'em out, and write what's in there. Then you put the bag on this here stretcher, and the transporters will take it to the vault. If their clothes be nasty, you can mark INCINERATE on the chart, right here. Don't worry about throwin' their clothes out, though. There be clean clothes for them when they go home. People donate 'em."

"Oh," she added, "don't forget to ask if their teeth be theirs. The nurse got to know that. If they're not theirs, give 'em a denture cup. If they be unconscious, the nurse got to remove their teeth and put 'em with their valuables. But the women can keep their wigs."

I caught on to the job quickly, and found myself finishing two charts to the other clerks' one. When Miss Graham asked in a most intimidating tone, "What's your rush, girl?" I slowed down. I liked Ward 35 and wanted to stay there, and I didn't want anyone questioning why I automatically came with Mrs. Anderson. That evening, no one did.

The following week, when I reported back to Ward 45, Mrs. Anderson told me we'd both been permanently transferred to Ward 35. "Are you sure I'm transferred, too?" I asked. After all, I'd just been hired a couple of weeks earlier to be a clerk on Ward 45. *Who would do the work on Ward 45?* I asked.

"That's not for you to worry about," she grinned. "I told 'em we's a team and they din't question me."

I had my doubts, but once again, I followed her downstairs, and nobody ever did question it. I had just turned 18, and by a stroke of fate, was one of the youngest employees on one of the most exciting wards of Cook County Hospital--Medical Admitting.

## ❖ 9 ❖

My third evening as a clerk on Ward 35 was my first without Mrs. Anderson. The admissions were less than usual. There wasn't as much to do. I noticed the bathrooms and the stairwell were filthy. When I worked at the golf club, I was expected to clean what was dirty. So I found the mop in the utility room, and began mopping the stairwell.

When Miss Graham returned from her break and saw me swishing that mop, she put her hands on her hips and blurted out, "Girl, when you applied for this job, did they tell you one of your duties was to mop the floor? If not, then why the hell you mopping the damn floor? You crazy or something?"

This was the most she'd ever spoken to me. After a brief pause, she continued, "You start mopping when it's slow, they'll make us all mop. And then they'll lay off the cleaning lady because they think the clerks have enough free time to clean the damn place. And next thing you know, we'll be scrubbing the toilets. Now is that something you want to be doing every time we have a few minutes to breathe? Sit down, girl. You got a few things to learn. And one of them is to do *your* job. And nothin' *but* your job. You hear?"

I heard, loud and clear. And when she called me 'girl,' it was said in a tone that clearly meant 'you stupid ass white girl.' But I found it difficult to be idle. From then on, if it was slow in the clerk's office,

I'd hang out in the back, on the ward, taking in all the pandemonium. I wondered if I'd ever understand what the nurses and doctors were doing and why they were doing it. I could never picture myself doing what those nurses did, yet they weren't much older than me. *Would three years of nursing school make me as competent as them*? I wondered.

After a few weeks on the job, when I was beginning to feel relaxed as a clerk, Mr. Abdul began mumbling under his breath. Mrs. Anderson was off that night as well. He mumbled about white slave masters and how he would have been an African king today if my white grandfather hadn't enslaved his.

At first I ignored him, thinking some white guy on the street had insulted him and I was a convenient scapegoat. But his racist mumbling continued all night.

"Malcolm X was right. All white people are devils and should be killed."

Finally Miss Graham, who treated Mr. Abdul with as much indifference as she did me, barked, "Shut up, Abdul," then called him a fool.

At 10 p.m., I'd had enough, and told them both I was taking a break. I ran down the stairs to the first floor and, fighting tears, entered Ward 15, the cardiac intensive care unit. I knew no one on Ward 15, and had never been down there. I entered the clerk's office where two middle-aged women welcomed me into their office and introduced themselves.

"You look like you seen your first dead body," said the first, whose nametag said Mrs. Blackley. "Or you just having a bad night upstairs?" Sensing my surprise that they knew who I was, they laughed and said, "You don't know us, but we heard all about you. Not too many white girls scrubbing floors at County. You already got a name for yourself, Carol. You can scrub the floors down here anytime." They both laughed.

"So tell us why you're so upset," asked the other clerk. I told them.

"You wouldn't be talking about Mr. Abdul now, would you?" asked Mrs. Blackley, her eyes sharing knowing glances with her fellow clerk.

"Do you know him?" I asked, worried that they might be good friends.

"Do we *ever* know him! We don't know what he's like with white clerks, but we can tell you what he's like with colored clerks, at least women ones. All that man talks about is how *we* have robbed *him* of *his* manhood by being disrespectful. He don't get any work done for all his whining. That fool's been all over County, and nobody can work with him. Got a screw loose."

I begged them not to say anything.

"Don't you worry," both assured me. "Every woman clerk at County got his number." I hoped I could trust them.

"If you ever feel bad again," one said, "just come down here. We'll treat you like family."

When I returned to work next week, Mr. Abdul's timecard was no longer in his slot. When I asked Miss Graham what had happened, she just shrugged. "Man gone crazy probably." And that was the last I heard or saw of him. It was the first and only time I ever experienced personally directed racism from a fellow employee at Cook County Hospital.

# ❖ 10 ❖

I continued to report to work as a clerk on the busy admitting floor three evenings a week. I prepared a chart for each patient as they arrived from the Emergency Room. Once on Ward 35, patients were thoroughly examined by a doctor, and had laboratory and other diagnostic procedures performed. Once stabilized, they were sent to their ward.

Patients on Ward 35 were acutely ill and had multiple problems. Typical complaints were swollen feet, severe shortness of breath, chest pain, seizures, sudden paralysis, coughing of blood, or urinating blood. A number were unconscious or too drunk to cooperate.

Most of the words I wrote on the charts each evening had been foreign to me a few weeks earlier, but I was getting better at matching the diagnosis with the patient. Patients with yellow skin and tight, swollen bellies were alcoholics with hepatitis or cirrhosis of the liver. Emaciated men with hollow eyes, sunken Adam's apples, gray skin, and a hacking cough were typically Skid Row alcoholics with tuberculosis.

Heavyset men and women suffering from shortness of breath and swollen feet had congestive heart failure (CHF). Those who arrived from the ER attached to a portable oxygen unit usually had myocardial infarction (MI) or pneumonia written in the diagnosis box. Patients with swollen faces who smelled like ammonia usually had some kind of kidney problem, or chronic renal failure (CRF).

On one particularly busy evening, the head nurse said she needed my help in the back. Seeing the confused look on my face, she said, "Don't worry. I'll show you what to do."

I followed her to the bedside of an unconscious man. A doctor was standing behind his head, squeezing a black rubber bellows. The bellows was attached to a tube that went down the man's throat, into his lungs. The tube was attached to a portable oxygen unit.

"Watch what the doctor's doing," said the nurse. "The patient can't breathe on his own. He should be on a ventilator, but there aren't any to spare anywhere in the hospital. So we have to breathe for him manually. You just have to squeeze the ambu bag eighteen to twenty times a minute. Do you think you can handle that?"

*It was clear the man would die if somebody didn't do it.* I took my place on the stool and began squeezing the bag. I counted my squeezes out loud for the first fifteen minutes, intensely concentrating on my task. For the next hour, I counted to myself and continued squeezing. My hands really hurt, but I couldn't stop.

From my stool, I had a direct view of the drug overdose room, packed to overflowing. That night, they were mostly heroin ODs. To my right, patients who had been rushed in with heart attacks and strokes just hours earlier occupied the four cardiac care beds.

An old woman in the corner slept peacefully, in a diabetic coma. I remembered trying to pry her shoes off earlier. They were too-small shoes that seemed glued to her swollen feet, pocked with smelly lesions. Her comatose state kept her from noticing the nauseous look on my face as I peeled off her socks.

As I counted and squeezed, counted and squeezed, I caught glimpses of the patients in the isolation rooms, both with suspected TB. Earlier in the evening I had to wear a mask when I checked their clothes—a protection against the stench as well as the disease. I had decided to send their excrement-caked clothes to the incinerator. New patients kept being wheeled in, on stretchers and in wooden wheelchairs. All needed a bed, even though there was 'no room at the inn.' Any other hospital would have hung a 'No Vacancy' sign up, but Cook County Hospital couldn't turn these patients away. County was the last resort.

My shift ended at 11 p.m. *Would I get relief*? I wondered. Perhaps one of the ventilator patients in the hospital would die in the next two hours, freeing the machine for this man. I didn't even know his diagnosis. *Who was this man? Did he have a family? Or did he roam the streets, one of the legions of homeless who passed through the County?*

I would never find out. At 10:30 p.m., the beeping noises coming from the cardiac monitor stopped. A doctor pushed me aside. The medical team took emergency action. For over thirty minutes, I stood with my back to the wall, watching as they performed CPR. They squirted jelly on his chest, shocked him with paddles, then injected medicine directly into his heart with a long needle. Their heroic efforts were unsuccessful and they covered his face with a sheet. Standing against the wall, I wondered what I'd done wrong. *Had I missed a beat? Had I squeezed too fast? Had I been too distracted?* This man's life had been left in my hands and I'd let him down. I had seen my first death, and I felt responsible.

As I shakily packed my things to leave, the head nurse, Mrs. Sanchez, ran over to me and asked to speak to me privately. I thought she was going to fire me on the spot. Instead, she asked if I would be interested in working in the back with the nurses from now on, as a student assistant instead of a clerk. She said I had been a great help that evening. I told her I still hadn't learned how to take a pulse or a blood pressure. I was just taking Chemistry and Microbiology courses all day—no nursing courses. She said she'd talk with an in-service instructor the next day to arrange some basic training for me.

As I walked back to my room through the musty tunnel, I felt so confused. A man had just died under my watch and I was being 'promoted.' Or was I just being 'promoted' because they were so overworked that *any* pair of hands could help. I thought about Mrs. Sanchez's offer. Learning a clerk's job was one thing, but learning how to be a nursing assistant in two days was positively frightening.

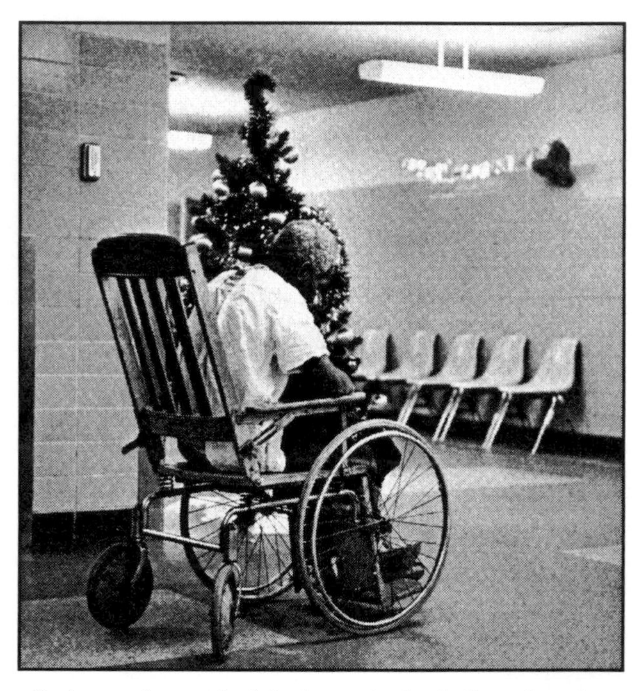

Patients often waited for hours in the halls to be taken to or picked up from the X-ray department.

# ❖ 11 ❖

Mrs. Sanchez told me that my basic training had been scheduled on a 'quieter' floor, Ward 28. Ward 28 was located on the second floor of the four-story B Building, the former psychiatric hospital. Steel bars still covered the windows. Each ward had beds for about 150 patients. The building was mostly filled with alcoholics going through withdrawal (DT's), alcoholics with hepatitis or ascites of the liver, or drug overdoses. At first glance, Ward 28 resembled a male maternity floor with all the men with tight swollen bellies waddling up and down the corridor.

I met the in-service instructor at the nurse's station and she gave me a brief tour of the ward. The beds were lined up parallel to each other, separated only by newly purchased green curtains. Each bed had a little nightstand for essentials.

In the sunroom at the end of the ward, patients could watch television, smoke and use the pay phone. The patients, some looking half dead, lined up in their wooden wheelchairs for that one phone.

"Mr. Smith!" barked a nurse to an elderly man in a wheelchair. The phone was cradled against his stubbled chin with one hand. His other hand was clutching his crotch. "You're on strict bedrest," yelled the nurse. "Who let you out of bed?"

"I'm just talkin' to my sugar," he protested. "No crime in that. Gimme another minute." Turning away from the nurse, he continued his phone conversation. The nurse shook her head and muttered under her breath. Then she directed the aide to wheel Mr. Smith back to bed.

"Din't I just say I was gettin' off the phone?" argued the irate patient, when the nurse's aide tried to pry the phone from his hands. "Well, I mean to, soon as I'm done here." He thrashed his arms, causing the IV tubing to swing wildly against his chair.

"Nurse!" yelled a patient halfway down the ward. "I need a nurse!" Thinking there was an emergency, my instructor ran down the hall to see what was wrong. I ran after her.

"I'm done with the bedpan," said the patient, a grossly overweight man with bulging, bloodshot eyes. Beads of perspiration rolled down his dark face. A large piece of white tape with the words "BEDREST" scrawled in black magic marker had been affixed to the foot of his bed.

My instructor reached under the sheet and grabbed the full, foul-smelling bedpan. She emptied its contents in the utility room. She then told the nurse that the patient in Bed Twelve had produced a "large amount of soft putty-colored feces."

"Is he on hepatitis precautions?" my instructor asked, alerted by the light color of his stool. The floor nurse nodded. "Then how come a 'Hepatitis Hazard' warning hadn't been taped to the end of the bed?" she asked, looking irate.

"OK, let's get started," my instructor said to me, after returning the bedpan.

"Have you ever taken a rectal temperature?" she asked, as she led me to the bed of an emaciated, comatose man. The blood vessels on his tight black forehead protruded like earthworms. I didn't have to say anything; the look on my face told her the answer.

"An alcoholic with liver failure," she noted, after quickly scanning his chart. His palms and soles glowed luminescent yellow, a common skin color on this floor. My eyes met those of the other patients—all yellow-tinged.

The thought of taking a rectal temperature on a stranger filled me with anxiety. I pulled the green curtain around his bed and stood on one side, waiting for guidance. My instructor rolled his body, pure dead weight, toward her. She told me to pull down the top sheet.

My anxiety turned to revulsion when I discovered a pool of diarrhea under him. I reeled back and pointed to the sheets, hoping she'd say, "Sorry about that. We'll find another patient." Instead, she seemed delighted at this unexpected bonus and urged me to proceed.

She asked if I'd ever made a bed around a comatose patient. I told her I'd never made *any* hospital bed before. I didn't tell her that I rarely had made my bed at home. And now that we had Sophie the maid, I never made my bed in the nurse's residence either. "What a perfect opportunity!" her smug smile seemed to say. So, I spent the next half hour bathing the man, changing the bed, and finally taking the rectal temperature. His unconscious state spared him my embarrassment.

My instructor then showed me how to record urinary output, how to put a bedpan under a patient, and how to remove it. She explained how to take special precautions with hepatitis patients. She also explained the behavior of a number of patients who were talking to themselves. They asked us to remove the bugs from their sheets. Or to swat the creatures on the walls.

"They're in DT's," she said. "Alcohol withdrawal."

Dinner break came as a welcome relief. When I returned after dinner, the sun had already set. Within a few minutes, all the lights went out on the ward, with one flick of the switch. "How do you see anything back here without lights?" I asked.

"You have to use flashlights," she explained.

"What if a patient wants to read?" I asked. She looked at me as if I were crazy to have asked that question. With the onset of darkness, it seemed that more patients began hallucinating. The place seemed like a mental hospital, with all the screaming and howling.

I told my instructor about a few of the drug overdoses I'd seen on Ward 35, and how frightening they had been to observe. Most of our admissions had overdosed on heroin or PCP, an animal tranquilizer also known as angel dust.

One fellow high on angel dust hyperventilated as if he were a train, choo-chooing slowly at first, then escalating his breathing to a feverish pace until his face was bright red and his muscles were so tense that the blood ran up his IV tubing. Then he'd pass out and go for minutes without breathing. Then, the choo-chooing would start all over.

After two evenings on Ward 28, my in-service instructor said I was ready to return to Ward 35 and start working with the nursing staff.

"What I've taught you is the tip of the iceberg, but it's enough to make you somewhat useful to the nurses. Good luck!"

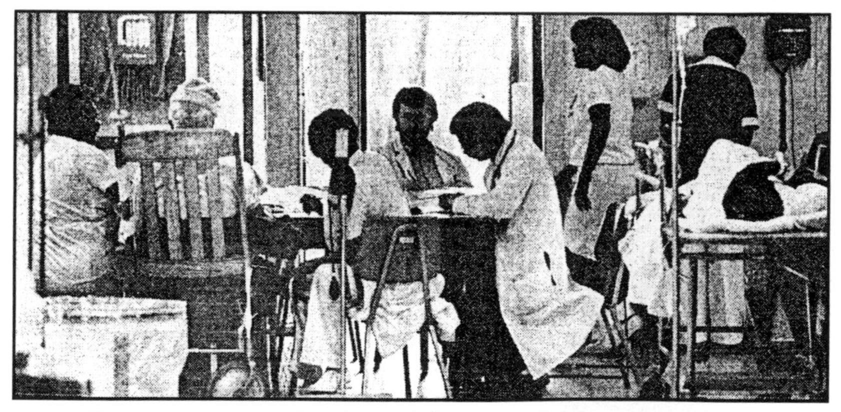

Doctors, nurses and patients sitting around the center table on Ward 35, also known as the Medical Admitting floor, one of the most hectic in the hospital. To transport critical patients from the ER to Ward 35 required two elevators and block-long walk through the tunnel. Patients were often lined up in wheelchairs and stretchers down the hall.

## ❖ 12 ❖

My first night back on Ward 35, Mrs. Sanchez asked me to assist the nursing staff and doctors wherever I was needed. Someone was always yelling for help and there never seemed to be enough. Even so, the evening nursing staff on Ward 35 provided top-notch care. They included four RNs, three LPNs, and three nurse's aides. Occasionally, there were student assistants as well.

The nurses raced non-stop all evening, handling each emergency like pros. Their hands were always filled with supplies or medications, as they carried on simultaneous conversations with several doctors, nurse's aides and technicians. All seemed to have eyes in the back of their heads, knowing who was climbing out of bed, having a seizure, pulling out an IV, or choking on saliva.

All four nurses were outspoken patient advocates. It was they who determined the moral code on the floor when it came to doctor/ patient relationships. If a med student or intern flubbed a procedure, they insisted his superior do it. If they felt a procedure or a medication was uncalled for, they'd speak to the doctor quietly outside the room. And the doctors listened. These nurses dealt with the same emergencies every night. If anyone knew what to do, it was the nurses.

Soon after I had arrived, I heard one of the Indian doctors yell from behind a curtain, "I need a nurse in Room 3."

"What for, Dr. Shah?" asked Mrs. Sanchez in her sing-song accent.

"A shpinal tap," he said. The doctor had a tray set up in the room to do the spinal tap. His hands were already gloved.

"Miss Karels will help you," she replied, and she called me over to Room 3. Outside the room, she whispered, "All you have to do is hold the patient in position. The doctor is going to numb the patient's back, then insert a needle to remove the spinal fluid. Come get me if he sticks the patient more than three times. Three sticks and you're out. That's our rule."

"OK, sir, put your knees up to your chin, as far as they will go," the doctor told the patient, an old grizzled man who looked confused but nevertheless did his best to follow the doctor's heavily accented instructions. "Now, sir, tuck in your chin—try to touch your knees. Good, good. Now, just hold him in that position, Nurse."

The doctor must have known I wasn't a *real* nurse, in my pink pinafore. But I stood on the side of the bed and held the patient in the position for what seemed like an eternity. I watched as the doctor probed the man's spine with his long fingers, then injected a medicine to numb the pain.

A few minutes later, he inserted a huge needle into the man's spine, wiggled it around, pulled it back, pushed it back in, then finally withdrew it completely. I exhaled, relieved that the procedure was over.

But it wasn't. The doctor's fingers continued to palpate the man's spine. A moment later, after saying, "one more little shtick," he inserted the needle again. The patient endured the procedure with grace, flinching as the needle entered his spine, but not questioning anything the doctor did to him.

After a moment, and an angry shake of his head, the doctor withdrew the needle again. I remembered what Mrs. Sanchez had said,

"Three sticks and you're out." *What would I do if the third stick didn't produce the desired spinal fluid?* Fortunately, the third stick was a bulls-eye, and the doctor withdrew two tubes of clear fluid.

"You lie flat now," he told the patient, "or you'll get a headache. Stay flat for an hour. Don't sit up for anything, not even to pass water." The old man obeyed.

## ❖ 13 ❖

With the exception of the belligerent drunks, the drug OD's, and the severely disoriented, the patients we admitted to Ward 35 were exceptionally polite and cooperative. They expressed gratitude for any care they received, even under the most stressful of conditions.

Most were older black men and women who had lived through Jim Crow laws and humbly accepted treatments without protest. After hearing what the doctors or nurses intended to do-- draw blood, start an IV, do an EKG--most responded by saying, "You do what you have to do, Nurse." And always "Thank God for the County."

Even after being stuck multiple times—for blood work, for a spinal tap or for an IV—they seemed to take it all in stride. When success was finally achieved, they'd whisper, "Thank the Lord. Thank you, Doctor." Or, "God Bless You, Nurse. I'm feeling better already."

It didn't take me long to realize that many of the patient's problems were the result of not understanding their disease. Or failure to take the proper dosage of the prescribed medicines.

"Have you been taking your medicine?" the nurse would ask.

"It ran out, Nurse," they'd apologize, "My grandkids been sick and I couldn't find the time to see the doctor to get another perscription."

Or... "I was feeling better, so I stopped taking my pressure pills." Or "I was feeling bad so I took two pills a day instead of one. That's why I ran out early." Or "I thought I was cured of the diabetes (or the TB)."

From what the doctors said, there was very little patient teaching going on in the clinics, and this was a concern of many staff members on Ward 35.

Miss Nixon poked her head in the room shortly after I finished labeling the test tubes with the spinal fluid. Cradled in her arms were two glass IV bottles and tubing.

"We need you in the overdose room, Carol," she said. "Dr. Patel needs help with a physical. The guy's drunk and his speech is really slurred, and Patel can't understand a word he's saying. And vice versa, I might add."

Entering the room, I heard Dr. Patel ask the patient for a urine specimen. "Please pass your warter into the receptacle," he said, handing the patient a small urine cup.

"Say what, man?" responded the obstinate patient.

"Here, he wants you to pee in the bottle," I said, giving him the larger urinal.

"Why dint he say so in the first place?" asked the patient, angrily pulling his penis out from under the sheet to comply with the doctor's request. I turned my head while he filled the urinal. I continued 'translating' for the rest of the physical.

Next, the nurse told me Dr. Johnson needed help in Room 1 with a GI (gastrointestinal) bleeder.

"He'll need an NG (nasogastric) tube and some iced saline for lavage," she told me.

*Say what?* Now I needed a translator. NG, GI and lavage were not in my vocabulary yet. But I went into Room 1 and asked the intern, a lanky American with red hair and a scraggly red beard, if he needed any help.

"Sure. Go get a basin of ice and a bottle of saline. When you get back, I'll show you what to do." So, for the next half hour, I performed what the nurse had called gastric lavage. I filled a turkey baster with iced saline, then squirted the salt water solution into an orange naso-gastric tube that connected the patient's nostril to his stomach. Then I released the pressure on the bulb to allow the stomach contents to flow back into the bulb. I then squirted the stomach fluid into a metal basin, grimacing the entire time. I kept doing that until the stomach contents were clear.

"Good job," said the doctor. "You can stop now. I'll hook him up to the GOMCO, a suction machine. I have to draw some more blood here."

I left Room One and stood in the hall for a few minutes, my own stomach in knots. I noticed that several new patients were lined up in wheelchairs in the hall, none with paperwork. I ran into the clerk's office and offered to help with the charts. The only clerks on duty that night were Mrs. Anderson and a new one named Fitz.

"Have a seat," said Mrs. Anderson. "We be missing you tonight. I be glad for the help." I had started working on a chart when Miss Collins, one of the nurses, walked into the clerk's office.

"What are you doing in here, Carol?" she asked.

"They're really backed up and they're short tonight," I explained, thinking I was doing the right thing. "I just came in to help."

"You can't do both," she said, in a stern voice. "You're either a clerk or a student assistant. But you can't be both." I apologized to Miss Collins. "Sorry," I whispered to Mrs. Anderson.

"It's OK," she grinned. "Be glad they need you more. You'll become a real nurse faster working with them than you will with me. Someday, you might even be my nurse. And I want you to be a good one."

# ❖ 14 ❖

Ward 35 was a revolving door of doctors and patients. Only the nursing staff remained constant. All of the interns at Cook County Hospital, regardless of their chosen specialty, had to rotate through the Medicine Department for at least two months, which meant they spent one night in three on Ward 35 admitting patients.

Future surgeons, ophthalmologists, pediatricians and psychiatrists—all sat around the central table on Ward 35, conferring with other doctors and the nurses while they worked up one new patient after another. Whenever they were unsure of what to do, they'd call in a consulting doctor. Therefore, at any given time in the evening, we had from ten to twenty doctors on Ward 35.

Whenever they were on call, the interns and residents were up for at least 36 straight hours. They weren't exhausted on Ward 35, but they would be by the following evening, after having been up all night admitting fifteen to twenty new patients.

At County, interns and residents in 1971 were primarily men. Interns conducted histories and physicals, drew their own blood samples, did their own diagnostic tests such as EKGs, inserted their own IVs, and transported blood work *and* patients if a transporter wasn't available. Tubes of blood, tourniquets, syringes, half-eaten doughnuts, pocket reference books and notecards filled the pockets of their white lab coats.

If these interns and residents, also known as the house staff, had wives, families, girlfriends or personal lives outside the medical center, they rarely, if ever, brought them up in conversation around the center table. As was true of the nurses, the hospital and its inherent dramas seemed to absorb their lives. Most lived in Karl Meyer Hall, ate all their meals in the Karl Meyer Dining Hall (doctors only), and rarely left the medical center.

I watched the new doctors try to figure out the personalities of various staff members. *Who's on your side? For whom do you do little favors? Who can you joke with? Who do you avoid like the plague?* Most were quickly relieved to see that everybody on Ward 35 was helpful and friendly.

Most interns had interests other than medicine and we shared many spirited conversations around the center table. Some were Communist sympathizers; others had fled Communist countries. Some were Vietnam veterans; others were Vietnam protestors. Some were Jesuits and conscientious objectors to the war; others were outspoken atheists.

What they all had in common was social activism and a desire to practice medicine. During the few quiet moments around the center table, I learned about the evils and the wonders of Communism, Socialism, the Catholic theology of liberation in Central America, Cesar Chavez's struggle for the migrant workers, Dorothy Day's Catholic Worker movement in New York City and the barefoot doctors of China.

Ward 35 was like being enrolled in a Master's Program on World Politics and Inner City Medicine. And I was the eager pupil, excitedly taking it all in and asking as many questions as I could.

In the weeks before Thanksgiving, Ward 35 had been total pandemonium. New admissions kept coming up from the Emergency

Room even though the hospital census was full.

"Why is the ER still sending patients up?" I asked Miss Nixon, observing that patients were lined up all the way to the elevator, in stretchers and wheelchairs.

One doctor overheard my question and responded, "We're having a 'heal-in.' We're filling the hospital to make a point that the private hospitals won't accept critically ill patients even when County is filled to capacity. We're trying to show how much red tape is involved in getting a patient transferred."

Another harried doctor, who'd just examined his fourth admission in three hours, piped in, "Nick's right. I'd like to see Dr. H and his administrator pals on the fourth floor spend some time in the ER making phone calls to other hospitals at midnight. Their goal is to decentralize County, maybe even close the place. But if nobody accepts County's patients, where the hell are they supposed to go?"

"Who's Dr. H?" I asked. Everybody looked at me as if I were crazy.

"He's the doctor who runs the hospital, the head of the Health and Hospitals Governing Commission," said the one named Nick.

"You must have seen him around—tall, elegant-looking, long sideburns, handle-bar moustache, always wears leather leisure suits. He's from Panama. He's never practiced medicine, but he's the highest paid public official in the state. If you ask me, all he's done to improve the place in the past year is paint the walls, scrub the floors, wash the windows and hang green curtains between the beds."

"Does he eat in the cafeteria?" I asked, thinking I had seen someone who met that description.

"No way!" they all laughed. "He and his entourage from New York City have a private dining room on the fourth floor. The only public place you'll see *them* is on the elevators, or on the nightly news."

Another added, "They ruined the hospitals in New York, so they recruited them to fix things here. My guess is their mission is to screw the place up so bad they'll have to close it."

I made a mental note to look out for this Dr. H. A few days later, his face made the front page of the *Chicago Sun-Times*. He had fired the head of the Department of Medicine and several residents with whom I had worked on Ward 35, including Nick, the 'ringleader' of the heal-in.

I learned about these firings in the newspaper. It was never mentioned in my nursing classes. It seemed the faculty of the nursing school had no idea what was going on in the hospital politically, or maybe they just saw no reason to share it with us.

After the firings, Ward 35 became the central gathering place for angry residents and interns to plan strategy and discuss their grievances. Sitting at the center table, writing my nurse's notes, I overheard many of these heated conversations and became increasingly nervous when many of the American doctors spoke openly about leaving.

"I'm off to Loyola," said one resident. "I really wanted to stay here and make a difference. But if the administration doesn't want to hear what we have to say, how can any of us make a difference? You speak up and you get fired. The doctors and nurses are the ones who know how this place should be run and what's needed, not a bunch of arrogant administrators and ward managers who are more concerned about the bottom line than health care."

Miss Nixon piped in, "If our contract negotiations don't go as planned, we're out of here too."

"They want to close the hospital?" asked an intern who looked more like an English bard with his shoulder-length greasy hair and goatee than a physician. "Well, let them close it. By my count, at least one hundred interns, residents and attendings are leaving after the first of the year, and, if enough of us leave, Dr. H won't have a choice but to close the place. But the only ones who will suffer are the patients. They certainly don't have the clout needed to keep this place open."

I'd only been at County three months but I now knew this was where I was meant to be and that, despite my lame reasons for enrolling in nursing school, I wanted to be a nurse. The profession was far different than I had ever imagined. These County nurses weren't handmaidens to doctors--they ran the show! I thought they just gave shots, but they assessed patients, evaluated their condition and relayed their suggestions to the doctors continually. The knowledge they had about so many conditions was unbelievable. There was so much to learn and I knew I was in the best place to get that knowledge--Cook County Hospital. For selfish reasons, I prayed the doctors and nurses would stay.

# ❖ 15 ❖

It seemed as if I were the only one in my nursing class who knew what was going on politically in the hospital. Nobody else seemed to know that the doctors were leaving en masse and that the hospital might close any day.

The main drama in *my* life was Ward 35. Yet the main drama for many of my classmates was just getting through their Microbiology, Chemistry and Anatomy classes. Nursing school was far more difficult than I expected. I had been an Honors student in high school yet my nursing courses were far more challenging. I knew I'd have to get through them too, as difficult as they were, if I wanted to remain at the nursing school.

I often daydreamed about Ward 35 during lectures. After drifting off during a lecture on the circulatory system, I refocused, only to notice a complicated drawing on the blackboard. It made me nervous that I didn't remember the instructor drawing it. I raised my hand to ask a question.

"I understand about veins taking blood to the heart and arteries taking blood from the heart," I began, "but I still don't understand what connects the two." As soon as I had asked the question, I realized that I knew the answer. But it was too late.

Immediately, Aaron, a classmate who already had a BS in

Chemistry, turned around in his chair and said, "Either you have been asleep for the past forty-five minutes or you haven't been listening to a word he said." His remark stunned me. I couldn't believe a fellow student could, or would, humiliate me, or anyone, in front of the entire class. My eyes welled up with tears.

The teacher just smiled, shook his head in comic disbelief, and said, "For your benefit, Miss Karels, and for the benefit of others who might have been dozing during my lecture, I'll quickly review veins, arteries *and capillaries*." I listened attentively this time.

After class, I made a mad dash for the bathroom so nobody would notice my reddened eyes. While in the stall, I heard the voices of two black students near the sinks. "You see how Aaron made that girl out to be a fool when she asked that question?" said one. "That ain't right. That's why nobody be askin' no questions."

The other one replied, "I didn't understand what he was talkin' about either. If she didn't ask that question, I still wouldn't know what in hell he was talking about. It's a shame how people be makin' you feel so stupid, just to make themselves look smart." Wide-eyed and open-eared, I remained in the stall, taking in their conversation. When I finally emerged from the stall, it was an awkward moment when they realized I'd overheard them.

"Nobody got no business talking to you that way," said one. "He should be ashamed of hisself." Then they walked away from me and returned to class.

My first opportunity to work alongside some of my black classmates was in December, during an Anatomy Lab where we had to dissect a cat. My partners were Kiki and Elaine.

Kiki had the face and body of a twelve-year-old. She reminded me of a junior Black Panther when she wore her Black Power T-shirts. She told me she was nineteen and had just graduated from high school. I remembered she seemed mildly militant at the beginning of school; now she just seemed nervous and insecure.

In contrast, Elaine was self-assured, stylish, and reminded me of Audrey Hepburn with an afro. The three of us walked over to the box of cats, all hard as loaves of stale French bread and smelling strongly of formaldehyde.

"Do you have any preference?" I asked the two as we nervously sorted through the box of stiff tabbies, calicos, black cats and orange cats—all of which had probably waited patiently for homes in shelters just weeks before.

"Just no orange ones," said Kiki, thrusting out her lower lip and making a face. "Reminds me of my own cat."

"I know what you mean," I said. "I have three at home. I think I'd rather be dissecting a human than a cat." They picked a black tabby that looked like my favorite pet, Missy, and laid it on the dissecting table, next to our scalpels, gloves and tweezers.

"I shoulda called in sick today and just gone home to be with my baby," said Kiki. "The last thing I want to be doin' today is cuttin' up some cat."

"Baby?" I asked.

"I got a little boy," she said. "He be two this Sunday."

"*You've got a kid?*" I asked, trying to hide my amazement at the fact that someone who looked as young as she had gotten pregnant. She must have weighed 80 pounds!

"Who takes care of him while you're at school?" I asked.

"My Grandma," she said. That's who I live with."

"You don't live in the nurse's residence?" I asked, thinking how hard it must be to commute, go to school *and* worry about a baby.

"I live here during the week, and I go home on weekends," she said. "Otherwise, I'd have no time to study. And if I don't pass, my Grandma's gonna kill me.

Elaine nodded, then said, "I know what you mean. I got a little girl at home myself—nine years old. Seems like everybody but me looks after her. I either been working or going to school or both since she was born."

Just then, our instructor walked by and advised us on how to make the initial incision into the cat and told us what organs to look for. He then handed Elaine some blank paper, saying we should draw each organ.

After he walked away, Elaine said, "You two can do whatever you want to that cat—I'm not touching it. When you find something interesting, just point it out, and I'll draw it as best I can."

I made the initial incision and as I did so, we all grimaced and shared disgusted looks. After a few minutes, we got into a comfortable routine, and I'd point out the organs as I found them.

"How you know that's the liver?" asked Kiki, when I pointed out the smooth organ.

"It looks just like the liver you find in the grocery store," I said. "See, it's dark red and has two lobes. It's just not shiny and moist like the ones you eat." Then we cut into the heart and tried to identify the valves. After a while, we began talking about things other than the cat's organs.

"What did you do before you came here?" I asked Elaine.

"After I got my degree in Psychology from DePaul, I was a Playboy bunny," she said.

"You're foolin', girl!" said Kiki, glancing with wide eyes at Elaine's flat chest. "Were you in the magazine?"

"No way, I'm not a fool enough to do that!" she laughed. "I just served drinks at the Playboy Club in Chicago. I wore one of those little bunny costumes that turned my 32A into a 36C with just a few wires and pads. False eyelashes, false uppers, false bottoms—and at least two false hairpieces, too!" she added. "It was just another uniform, and Lord knows I've worn my share of different uniforms."

"So you left the Playboy Club for *this place?*" I asked.

"You think I want to spend the rest of my life as a Playboy bunny?" she scoffed.

Just then, Kiki excused herself to go to the bathroom, saying she felt sick. When Kiki was out of earshot, I asked Elaine if she and Kiki were good friends.

"Not really," she said. "I've talked with her a few times. She was part of the summer program and those kids mostly stick together. If you ask me, this school screwed with their minds by bringing them all here for the summer, giving them false hopes, and then sendin' half of them home like they're trash because they didn't pass the entrance test. The school hired all those psychologists and tutors to help, but some of these kids barely passed high school. And then you've got the rest of the class who already have degrees and careers."

Until then, I knew little more than what Genelle had told me about this summer program. I had been so wrapped up in the politics on Ward 35, that I didn't know anything about the politics in my own class! I really felt bad for Kiki, who had so much pressure on her to succeed. And I felt for Elaine, who seemed to breeze through her studies, but rarely had an opportunity to see her child. They had *real* reasons to become nurses. They had children dependent on them, counting on that nursing paycheck three years down the road. I decided it was best not to tell them what was going on in the hospital. Pass or flunk, perhaps we'd all be gone after the first of the year if things continued as they did.

# ❖ 16 ❖

A few weeks after the dissection lab, we took our final exams for the first trimester. Confident that I had passed, I took my first airplane trip, to California. I had saved enough money from working on Ward 35 to purchase the plane ticket. I stayed with cousins who had just moved out there from the midwest.

We all piled into a VW bug, drove up to Mammoth Mountain, checked into a chalet covered with six feet of snow, and I took a real ski lesson. I had taken some lessons at the golf club, on glare ice, but was totally unprepared for mountains of fluffy snow.

After a few days in the mountains, I became caught in the spell of the outdoors, the smells of pine trees and chimney smoke and the exhilaration of learning how to downhill ski. I forgot about the drama I'd left behind.

When I returned to school a week later, reality quickly set in. Less than half the students in my class showed up. From an initial 150 students, we were down to 70! An equal number of blacks and whites remained. Just two Hispanic girls remained, and only four of the eleven men.

I was told just as many dropped out as had failed, perhaps deciding that nursing school just wasn't their cup of tea. Perhaps I might have been among them, had I not gotten a preview of things to come on Ward 35.

"Maybe they're the lucky ones," said Genelle, about those who didn't return. "They got out before disaster struck. Julio just called and said a lot more docs are threatening to resign. And if they do, how can the hospital stay open?" Julio was her fiancé, a Fellow in the Department of Medicine.

"How many doctors *have* resigned?" I asked, hoping my favorites on Ward 35 weren't among them.

"It's hard to say. They're all mad as hell at Haughton and the Governing Commission," she said. "Now the Commission has hired 'business administrators' to make decisions about when patients should be sent home. They set time limits for each type of disease and make the doctor justify each day he keeps a patient over the allotted days. That kind of thinking doesn't make any sense here. These patients come in with so many problems—they're just not your typical sick patients. They're malnourished so they don't heal well. They have TB, diabetes or high blood pressure on the side."

"Maybe the state is threatening to withhold funds if they don't follow these new rules," I suggested.

"Nah, it's much more than that," she said. "So much of it is political. This place has always stayed open so politicians could provide patronage jobs to their workers. Elevator operators, laundry workers, cooks, machinists, nurse's aides. Now that patronage hiring is illegal, there's no incentive to pour money into this place. I think their real objective is to phase out Cook County Hospital and force community hospitals to accept these patients. So the administration is doing everything it can to keep the census down, keep staffing down, things like that. They probably *want* the doctors to resign."

A few weeks later, in mid-January, about one hundred American doctors resigned and the hospital was on shakier ground than ever. But nothing was discussed in school and classes went on as usual.

At the end of May, the traditional capping ceremony was held. The females all donned our below-the-knee blue pinafores and white aprons for the first time. It was the first time many of us laughed together, as we all struggled to pin the organza cap, unique to County students, to our heads for the first time. The caps were clearly designed in the days when women piled their long hair into a neat bun at the top of their heads and covered it with the cap. Those of us with short hair and/or towering afros cursed and laughed at the absurdity of the situation. And of course, the men students didn't have to wear them, which made the capping ceremony even more absurd. The ceremony included the traditional tea served in china cups from silver pots.

In June, another hundred American doctors resigned the day after Genelle's nursing class graduated. Many of the graduates accepted positions at Cook County Hospital, despite predictions that the hospital would close any day.

During the summer, we took 'Introduction to Nursing' courses, covering many of the areas I had been introduced to on those two evenings on Ward 28—bedmaking, waste disposal, hygiene, vital signs, reading charts, nursing care plans, pharmaceutical terminology, etc. We also visited several areas of the hospital, including the Operating Room, the Recovery Room and the Delivery Room. The only area that was air conditioned was the Recovery Room.

In August, it was time to begin our Internal Medicine rotation. Our instructors broke us into groups of ten students. I had been assigned to Ward 55. My clinical instructor, Mrs. Wyckoff, seemed friendly and competent even though it was her first time teaching.

Each day, she assigned us to a patient and expected us to learn about his or her diagnosis and medications. Every morning, we submitted a care plan—a detailed outline of the patient's history, medical problems, and nursing care requirements. It often required hours of work in the evenings, depending on the severity and complexity of the patient's condition. She drilled us on our patient's medications, their side effects, the nature of their illness, the functions of the organs involved and the recommended treatment. We then cared for the patient until noon, giving bed baths, making the bed, dispensing the medications and teaching patients about their respective diseases. I had been so used to the fast pace of Ward 35 that I worried I'd be bored spending an entire morning with just one patient. I need not have worried.

My first patient was named Kenny. He had been admitted from a nursing home with a urinary tract infection and bedsores. I had taken care of a few nursing home patients on Ward 35. Most had been grossly neglected in the home and then dumped at County when they developed medical complications. Kenny sounded like a dump.

Kenny was in an isolation room at the front of the ward. (Each ward had one or two isolation rooms for the sickest patients or those with contagious diseases). I found a pale, emaciated man-child lying in the fetal position in bed. Spittle dribbled from the corner of his mouth. His cracked red lips and red hair provided the only color on his body. His watery blue eyes were staring into space; his mouth and tongue moved as if they were chewing. I walked up to him. "Kenny?" No response. He just kept chewing and staring into space. His elbows were bent at a severe angle. I tried to straighten them out. Impossible. He had severe contractures from the lack of exercise, for months, maybe years. He had a feeding tube.

The room had a strong, nauseatingly sweet smell. There were so many different smells in that hospital. I'd already become familiar with the unmistakable smells of bloody diarrhea, kidney failure, diabetic comas, TB phlegm, unwashed bodies, clothes that hadn't been removed for a year, purulent sores and bleeding ulcer breath. I didn't recognize this smell. I lifted the sheets, expecting to find the same type of contractures on his legs, and perhaps some diarrhea in the bed. He had a urinary drainage bag hanging at the side of the bed. Both knees were bent up almost to his chin, and I noticed a huge dressing on his hip. I asked the busy nurse why he had the dressing.

"Bad, bad bedsores. The doctor have to come and clean it. Maybe tomorrow."

"Is that what smells?" I asked. She nodded.

"You take care of him tomorrow?" I nodded.

"He's very difficult patient," she began. "Starts crying, yelling if you move him. Can't even put him in a wheelchair. He won't get better here."

"Does he go for physical therapy?" I asked.

"No way!" she responded. "He cry too much with every touch. You see tomorrow."

The next day, my first day on the wards, we all went to our assigned patients. Just as I began bathing him, a consulting surgeon arrived to debride, or clean out, the bedsore. As most of my fellow students had never seen a bedsore, my instructor gathered us around to watch the procedure. The surgeon removed the dressing, revealing a black patch the size of a pie pan. Blackish-green jelly oozed out of one corner. The surgeon, clean-cut and wearing a tie, began cutting away the black tissue with a scalpel and scissors.

"He can't feel a thing," he assured us. "This is all dead, necrotic tissue."

With the first cut, foul-smelling black jelly oozed out. The nauseating smell overpowered the hot room.

"Putrified skin," said the surgeon. "This is a crime. That nursing home should be put out of business."

He continued cutting the dead skin, revealing a massive cavity in Kenny's sacrum, exposing the hipbones. Occasionally during the procedure, Kenny grunted, thrusting back his head like a bleating lamb. The severity of his contractions prevented him from hitting and kicking. "Almost done here, Kenny," said the surgeon.

When the procedure was over, the surgeon cleansed it with an astringent solution and then applied Maalox and sugar to the wound, followed by a dressing.

"Maalox?" I asked, remembering my Dad took it for his frequent stomachaches.

"Believe it or not, that's the recommended treatment for bedsores," he said. "They seem to heal faster. But the *best* treatment is maggots. They keep the wounds clean and release enzymes that promote healing. Natural healers have known it for years."

He wrote orders for the nurses to clean the sore three times a day. "Leave it open to air most of the time to promote healing. I'll debride it every few days. That bedsore's a beaut though, and it'll be a long time healing. Poor guy." Then he patted Kenny on the head.

It took forever to bathe him, turn him, exercise his limbs, make his bed and change his dressing. Though he asked for nothing, his needs were clear. I wondered what kind of care he received in the nursing home. I wondered what type of care he got at County, when nursing students weren't around to help. *I wondered how anyone could spend an entire life like that.*

# ❖ 17 ❖

Working on the wards from seven to noon changed the whole pace of nursing school. After lunch, we took courses such as Medical/Surgical Nursing, Nutrition and Pharmacology. We also took Sociology classes a couple of days a week at Loop College downtown. Going to school year-round, with only a week off between trimesters, was taking its toll. We had a tremendous amount of homework every night, including care plans for our patients, which were like medical research reports. Many students complained about the sudden surge in homework. Working three evenings a week in the hospital, from 3 to 11, I especially felt the burden.

My classmates were mostly upset with the homework assigned by our nutrition teacher, one new to the school. When this new teacher lectured at the podium, she reminded me of a judgmental preacher, preaching that the reason that so many of the patients at County were sick was because 'they don't pay no mind to their nutrition.' Fried chicken, whiskey, sweets, junk food, fried anything—they were all sins that the patients were now paying for. As student nurses, she told us, it was our mission to bring the gospel of nutrition to the patients who didn't know how to eat properly and to teach them how to prevent illness through good nutrition.

After one particularly confusing lecture, which resulted in a huge homework assignment on the Krebs cycle, Homan, the class radical, erupted. "Mrs. Collard, you driving us all crazy with this nutrition shit. You make it seem like that's all we got to study. We're here to be nurses, not nutrition experts." Homan had no respect for traditional teacher/student boundaries.

"Young man!" she shrieked. "Nobody speaks to me like that! Get out of my classroom *at once*!" she ordered. For a moment, I thought she was going to yank his afro and drag him out of class. Instead, it became a showdown, with both staring angrily at each other.

She then returned to the front of the class and said, " Y'all think you just got to know about heart attacks and strokes. Well, listen up. You gotta know your nutrition. And if you don't pass my class, or if you get expelled for what you just pulled, you never gonna be a nurse!"

After class, Homan and a group of angry black students banded together in the lounge. "They can't expel *all* of us. They need to expel *her* black butt."

The next day, a letter circulated among my classmates announcing that the students were going on strike against the nutrition teacher. They had hired a substitute teacher, a County nursing graduate with a Masters Degree in Nutrition. Apparently she had tutored a lot of summer program students. The alternative nutrition class would meet in the lounge, adjacent to the classroom. All students were invited to attend, we were told.

Clearly, the entire class felt the nutrition teacher was out of line with her demands. *But a strike against the teacher?* We all knew attendance was mandatory. If we missed two classes, we could be kicked out. *But would they expel the entire class?* Our class was united, and attended the alternative class in the lounge. We signed the attendance sheet, and did the homework assigned, for two days.

Even though the substitute did a good job, and the students begged her to stay on forever as our nutrition teacher, we all knew 'the strike' wouldn't last. On the third day, Mrs. R, the Acting Director of our school, addressed our class. Unlike the previous director who had retired to sell fine china at Marshall Fields, Mrs. R was a County grad. She was big and black and my classmates didn't intimidate her in the least. When *she* spoke, she commanded attention.

"You know I could expel all of you for this," she announced. "Clearly, you all have a lot to learn before you become nurses. You think you can just walk out when an assignment's too hard, or your patients or staff are uncooperative or you don't have the equipment you need? This is the County, kids. This place makes great demands on you and if you can't even handle an assignment on the Krebs cycle, well maybe you shouldn't be here."

Only *I* knew that the nurses in the hospital didn't share her philosophy. In fact, a nursing strike was brewing. In the weeks before Christmas 1972, both nurses and doctors were agitating for change. Conditions had been deteriorating steadily, especially after so many American residents and attending physicians had resigned earlier in the year. A new Chairman of the Department of Medicine, Dr. Quentin Young, had been hired to raise morale and help recruit new interns. He had done his own residency at County in years past.

Sitting around the center table, the doctors and nurses passionately discussed the deficiencies in the system—the insensitive administration, frozen salaries, staffing shortages, inadequate conditions, the hiring freeze, the lack of supplies and emergency equipment, inadequate delays in getting X-rays and lab results, the frequent disappearance of personnel and the breakdown of discipline, order, and morale in the hospital.

The nurses were especially upset because the administration now threatened their hard-earned contract. The three County-grad RNs who worked the evening shift on Ward 35 were active in the Illinois Nurse's Association. They spent much time during the day negotiating a new contract. They often arrived to work angry and disgusted after a particularly frustrating round of contract discussions. I knew nothing about contracts, labor relations or negotiations. I found their discussions both confusing and intriguing. The doctors also expressed interest in the nurses' grievances, as they closely paralleled their own.

Within weeks after negotiations with the Health and Hospitals Governing Commission began, the RNs unanimously voted to go on strike. The LPNs voted to join them, and in early November 1972, 1200 nurses picketed peacefully in front of the hospital. The RNs encouraged the students to join them on the picket line, and so, weeks after our aborted nutrition strike, we students were out on the streets carrying makeshift signs declaring "Student Nurses Support County Strike."

During this time, Mom visited to have lunch with me in the cafeteria. The head of the Volunteer's Office joined us. She asked if I supported the strike. I told her I did. She seemed furious with my answer and asked how I could ethically support such an action that would leave patients without caretakers. She said nurse's top priorities should be patients, not how much money they made.

She was a privileged white woman from the suburbs who ran the Volunteer Department. She always wore stylish clothes and hairdos, and I couldn't picture her doing the type of work that nurses did. I told her the nurses weren't striking for more money but for better working conditions. I told her that what they were striking *for* would benefit the patients more than anything.

"But you're nurses! You take an oath to care for people, don't you? And the fact that you chose to work here means you should be prepared to deal with shortages and other problems not found in private hospitals," she raged. "You should all be ashamed of yourselves."

Mom responded immediately. If there was one emotion Mom couldn't tolerate, it was guilt, and this woman was trying to lay an undeserved guilt trip on the hardworking nurses of County Hospital.

"I think Carol knows as much as anybody about what's going on in the hospital. She's been working there three nights a week and I'm shocked at some of the things she tells me. There aren't emergency carts on the floors. Nurses often work two shifts because there's not a pool of nurses to pick from if people call in sick. Maybe the patients will be better off in the long run if these nurse's grievances are addressed. I trust what she tells me, and if she wants to support their strike, I'm all for it."

I kept recalling Mrs. R' scolding after our nutrition strike. She warned us that nursing would be challenging, that we should be prepared for anything, and to just deal with it as professionals. She had also said that action shouldn't be taken until grievances had been aired with the administration. The nurses *had* done that, but they felt their grievances fell on deaf ears.

After Mom left, I joined some fellow students on the picket line with my sign. I noticed several television and newspaper cameras in the area, but hadn't been aware that my own picture had been taken until the next day, when Mom called and said, "Did you see you made the front page of the afternoon *Daily News?*"

"I'm not surprised," I replied, knowing that the nursing strike would get much media attention.

"No, I mean *you*, not the striking nurses. Your picture is on the front page. Go out and get a copy," she told me.

Immediately, I ran down to The Greeks and picked up a copy. Sure enough, my face occupied the front and center of page one, under the headline, 'Nurses Walk Out at County Hospital.' The photo showed me holding my sign and conversing with two other nursing students. An editor mistakenly captioned it 'Striking Nurses March Outside County Hospital Entrance on Harrison Street.' The photo depicting the picketing nurses appeared on the back page, with the caption, 'Nurses and student nurses discuss the decision to strike at County Hospital.' Somebody had goofed. The photo of the 1,200 marching nurses would have been far more appropriate on page one than a couple of student nurses talking to each other. But who was I to protest? I'd made the front-page news!

The strike lasted four days and neither side appeared happy with the outcome. A week later, I heard rumors that the administration was threatening layoffs. I hoped they were only rumors. Getting laid off would be a personal disaster; I couldn't live with the thought of not working on Ward 35. Yet days after the strike ended, I received a letter from the Personnel Department of the Health and Hospitals Governing Commission. I opened it slowly, dreading the contents.

*Dear Ms. Carol Karels:*
*It is with regret that I must inform you that because of the persistent reduction in average daily census and the consequent need to lower costs, the Health and Hospitals Governing Commission finds it necessary to reduce the work force at Cook County Hospital. You will be laid off effective December 15, 1972 at the end of your regularly assigned shift.*

I ran over to Karen's room and asked if she had been laid off, too. "We've *all* been laid off—all the student assistants," she told me. "And about a thousand others. No nurses or doctors—but LPNs, lab technicians, transporters." She reached over to get a copy of the *Daily News* from her bed, hot off the afternoon press.

"Look," she said, "The layoff made the headlines: 'Crisis Builds at County in Firings'—Story on Page 3." On page three, the headline read 'County Doctors Back Fired Workers.' We read the article together, which described how the Residents and Interns Association was protesting the layoffs, saying the staff of the hospital should be increased, not decreased.

Karen flipped the pages to the Want Ads section. "Check this out. A holiday greeting from the Commission!" I began reading the six-inch ad that began:

*"Seasons Greetings and Attention Employers: Cook County Hospital has many employees who will be available on 12-15-72. Qualified employees, skilled in various hospital classifications, having talents and potential for other types of jobs. They currently hold positions as LPNs, food service technicians, attendants, clerks, lab techs, custodial workers and lab assistants."*

*Two weeks before Christmas!* Economic necessity kept popping up as the reason. Yet it didn't make sense to me. Medical admissions overflowed each night. As far as I knew, the medical floors were filled to capacity. RNs and LPNs frequently worked double shifts. Transporters were in short supply. And if doctors waited hours now for lab results, what would happen after the layoffs? None of it made any sense.

# ❖ 18 ❖

Cook County Hospital was like a city unto itself, with every ward being a distinct neighborhood with its own politics, personalities and dramas. The Public Relations Department published a quarterly newsletter that focused on the positive aspects of the hospital: *County Softball Team Has Perfect Season. Burn Unit Nurses Honored. Chief of Cardiac Surgery Commended for Work with Children. Trauma Unit Lauded for Ingenuity. Laundry Workers Have Barbecue to Celebrate Co-Workers Anniversary.* An outsider would think County was one big happy family.

Being on the wards, day in and day out, we nursing students often saw a different picture. The County family, in many respects, was a very dysfunctional one, primarily because a distinct racial hierarchy existed among the staff.

The 1970's were a transitional time, but in 1973, doctors at County were primarily white or Indian men. The RNs were predominantly County-trained (white and black) or Filipino immigrants. The LPNs and nurse's aides were primarily black, as were the transporters, dietary workers, clerks and housekeepers.

On the wards, I occasionally witnessed clashes between the nurses and the aides over patient assignments. On one of my first days on the surgical floor, the Filipino RN had just handed out the assignments, after taking report from the night shift. Immediately, one of the aides started yelling in a threatening voice, loud enough for everyone, including the patients, to hear.

"This assignment ain't fair! How come you give Hudgins six 'up and abouts' and I only got three?" (Up and abouts were patients who were ambulatory and didn't require as much care.) "You think that's fair? And how come you gave me Jenkins again? I had my fill of that man, goin' on six days now."

"You only had Mr. Jenkins for four days," explained the frustrated nurse. "I have it here in my book. And Mrs. Hudgins has two full baths and two who need total assistance with feeding. Stop complaining. Go do your work."

"No! I'm telling you it ain't right!" responded the aide, raising her voice again. "Don't go tellin' me mines are easier. You ever try to feed Washington? That man takes all day to eat and I ain't givin' up my break for him today. And Greeley need help getting out of bed and walking to the bathroom, and I done told you about my back."

After verbally sparring in this way for several minutes, the nurse said, "You want I call the supervisor?" With that, the aide grudgingly accepted her assignment and walked off, muttering under her breath, "I been doing this shit since before she was born. Just who do she think she is, telling me my job? I should be makin' her money."

Later, while I was helping my patient with his breakfast, the patient named Mr. Washington called out to the still griping aide for help.

"I ain't missin' my break cuz of you again!" she responded, not even asking to see what he needed. We'd only been on the floor for forty minutes.

"Can't you just roll up my head so I can eat?" he pleaded. "It don't make no sense that you have to go on break before I'm set up to eat. Now my food's gonna get cold. They gonna take my tray away 'fo you get back."

"Who you to complain?" asked the aide as she headed toward the break room. "You ain't payin' nothin', so you ain't got no right to complain 'bout nothin'."

My classmate Shavonne caught the last of this conversation, and before the aide was out of sight, she rolled the head of the man's bed up, so he could begin eating. "People like her ain't got no business working at the County," said Shavonne to the patient, a grizzled old man in need of a shave. "She should be ashamed of herself, treating her own people like that."

"You got that right," said the old man. "She got some nasty attitude for a nurse. If you can't get treated right here, where can you go? Don't make no sense."

"Amen!" said Shavonne. "Problem is, I seen too many of them like her working here."

Later, when I went into the break room, I found most of the aides sitting in there. They were drinking coffee, squirting ketchup on their egg sandwiches and sharing their mutual tales of personal suffering. In those few moments I spent in the room, I heard them complain about the nurses and their ailments. Bad backs, arthritis, high blood pressure, ulcers, female problems. And they shared their problems at home, with their men, their children and their grandchildren. None seemed in any hurry to return to the patients.

I wondered how many years these women had collectively worked at the County. Although I wasn't sympathetic to them, I realized that the work they did was exhausting. Perhaps doing it for too many years could harden you, especially if you'd never had a break from it and if you didn't get any recognition.

I knew I'd make a good nurse someday. But I doubted I could handle the verbal abuse that so many nurse's aides and other help dished out to the RN's, doctors and patients on the surgical floors. And the 'it's not my job' attitude seemed endemic to many areas of the hospital.

"It just comes with the territory," my instructor said, shrugging, when I expressed my concerns. "You don't see County-trained nurses having these staff problems. It's mostly with the Filipino nurses, because of cultural and language differences. They don't have people skills."

The constant bickering over assignments, the belligerent attitudes, the disappearing acts—all seemed so out of place in a hospital where caring should have been the top priority. To me, County should have been a mecca of compassion, a melting pot of cultures, a place where caring came before economics and politics and color. But in contrast to the compassion and camaraderie I experienced on Ward 35, other areas of the hospital had too many callous and cranky crones like these who viewed themselves, not the patients, as the victims. They were clearly burned out and ineffective caretakers, yet whenever there was a layoff, the young, energetic and idealistic aides got the boot while those who were cooked were forever spared due to seniority.

## ❖ 19 ❖

Like my fellow students, the surgical nursing instructors seemed oblivious to the political crisis in the hospital. As long as there were patients who needed to be cared for, they were going to teach. There was never discussion about hospital politics.

"You ain't seen nothin' yet," joked my friend Karen. "When you finish your surgical rotation, you'll feel like a real nurse." I already felt like a real nurse. And I thought I knew it all. But in the next sixteen weeks, a new, even more challenging world revealed itself.

The biggest difference between the medical floors and the surgical floors were the *wounds* and the *wards. The surgical wards were huge,* with the nurse's station at one end and the last patient on the ward a full city block away. With the beds lined up next to each other, there must have been sixty patients on each ward. The wards in the main building, with all the old wooden wheelchairs lined up, reminded me of the turn-of-the-century TB sanitariums I'd read about in history books.

Each general surgery ward had a sterile dressing and treatment room where the patients were wheeled to have their dressings changed. No dressings were ever changed in bed. Since most post-op patients required pain medications and there were no call buttons, there was a lot of yelling of 'Nurse' on the wards. The patients on the surgical floors were often much younger and more assertive than those on the medical floors. “Nurse! Nurse! I need a Nurse! Where’s the nurse? I’m in pain!” There were always nurses on the floor to respond, but the timing of their response often depended on the attitude of the patient.

In those weeks, we learned everything possible about wound care from veteran County instructors who seemed to live and breathe surgical nursing. They were the best and left no detail unnoticed. Like our medical instructors, they grilled us each morning on our patient’s disease, their surgical procedures, their medications and side effects, and the function of the diseased organ(s). They watched us clean and dress the wounds in the dressing room, insisting we use absolutely sterile technique.

Five mornings a week, we arrived on our assigned ward at 7 a.m. sharp, and listened to the morning report, always given, it seemed, by an exhausted Filipino charge nurse. My instructor told us that many Filipino nurses worked two jobs, and sent all their wages back home to their families in the Philippines. Most lived in the nurse’s residence, paying $40 a month rent, and seemed to have no social life outside of the holiday parties held on the wards—soul food feasts that weren’t complete without Filipino pansit and egg rolls.

We spent intense weeks on the following wards: Neurosurgery, Vascular Surgery, Plastic Surgery, Urology, Orthopedics, ENT (Ear, Nose and Throat), the Surgical Intensive Care unit, the Recovery Room, the Emergency Room and the Burn Unit. The only place we didn’t go was the Trauma Unit.

There were so many different issues to deal with in surgery, so many different types of patients, so many complications and so many moral issues.

While doing a two-week rotation on the Neurosurgery ward, I was assigned to an eighteen-year old prisoner who had been shot in the spine about a month earlier. I remembered him from the day my class had spent in the Recovery Room. There, he had been wheeled in from the operating room, still on a respirator, connected to chest tubes, nephrostomy tubes and IV tubes.

Most surprising was that all four of his limbs remained shackled to the bed and he had an armed guard at his bedside in the Recovery Room, despite the fact that he was paralyzed from the waist down. I asked the recovery nurse assigned to his care, "Why the shackles and the guard? How can he possibly escape in that condition—unconscious and paralyzed?"

"You just can't take chances. I know it looks ridiculous and he's going nowhere, but state law requires this kind of security with *all* prisoners. He even had them on in the OR. It's a pain in the ass dealing with the damn things, but you'd be surprised how many prisoners have escaped from this place, guards or no guards. And even though this patient is paralyzed, friends have been known to come in and whisk a patient away."

I had never cared for a prisoner before. I recalled my feelings about my classmate Tammi's patient on the Ear, Nose, and Throat ward weeks earlier, an older man with cancer of the tongue. His tongue protruded from his mouth like a piece of raw liver; he drooled constantly, and had no control over the movement of the tongue. He required tube feedings because he couldn't swallow properly, and he had to write everything down, as he couldn't speak.

Tammi spent half the day wiping away saliva, giving him pain medications, and comforting him with back rubs. I noticed how demanding he was, shaking his head angrily and grunting if he didn't like something she did, scribbling furiously on his pad. Then I learned that he had been convicted of selling drugs to schoolchildren. He had served time in prison, a little over a year. Now a free man, he was dying a slow and painful death.

On the Orthopedics floor, at least ten of the patients on the floor were prisoners, and each had a guard assigned to him. "Why are there so many prisoners up here?" I asked the charge nurse.

"They break legs escaping from the police," she explained. "That's how they get caught—jumping out windows or getting shot in the leg. They bring them all here."

I assumed most prisoners would be tough-looking guys who never cracked a smile. Yet they were all friendly—laughing and joking with their guards and flirting with their caretakers. "Hey, sugar," yelled one to a young LPN passing by. "I'm gonna need lots of lovin' when I get out of here."

The LPN just laughed. Minutes later, the same prisoner yelled out a similar line to a student nurse. "Please tell me you gonna give me my bath today."

As friendly as they were, I quickly came to realize they were all con artists. They conned the doctors into increasing their pain medications and the nurses into giving it before it was time. They conned dietary workers for more food, and conned their guards to unshackle them at times. They were masters at intimidation and manipulation.

On the Orthopedic floor, I was assigned to an Irishman from Skid Row who had a fractured right femur. He looked like a leprechaun, with ruddy cheeks, a full head of red hair, an upturned nose and a thick brogue. Apparently, he'd fallen down some stairs while drunk. He had been operated on two days earlier and his right leg was now full of steel pins, suspended in the air with ropes and pulleys.

Providing nursing care to Orthopedics patients in traction could be quite challenging, since you had to move them, bathe them and change their position with great care. I never got the hang of traction.

But on the second day, my patient provided me with a unique nursing challenge: he went into alcoholic withdrawal. I imagined the stimulus he must have been receiving with his leg hanging in the air, supported by ropes and pullies, covered by a white sheet. As I stood next to his bed one morning, he yelled in a thick brogue, "By Jesus, get 'im miss. Whaderya jist standin' around fer?"

"Get what?" I asked, wondering what he had just seen.

"The little men, lass! Can't you see 'im, crawling all over me legs? Oh Jesus, Mary, Mother of God!" he screamed. And he leaned forward, lifting his hand as if to swat a fly off his leg.

"Goddamnittohell! You fuckers get outta here before I murder your little arses," he screamed as he waved his arms and violently rocked his own "arse" in bed, the only movement he was capable of making. Watching him, I thought he looked like a sailor on a ship in a stormy sea, hanging on top of the mast and screaming bloody murder to all who could hear him.

Several times a day, he screamed, "Gotta piss. Gotta piss now!" I'd give him the urinal, reminding him that it always hung at this bedside, that he could use it whenever he liked.

"I told you, lass, I ain't pissin' in no bottle." Getting him to use the bedpan for bowel movements was equally impossible. He'd yell so that the entire ward could hear, "Don't be stickin' that thing under me!"

Halfway through our Orthopedics rotation, we arrived on the ward one morning to find that all the bed curtains had been removed for cleaning.

"How can they do that?" I asked. "That's so demeaning!"

The head nurse laughed, "We didn't even have curtains a year ago! That's one of the few good things Dr. H initiated."

## ❖ 20 ❖

On the Urology Ward, I cared for an elderly Italian man, Mr. Caruso, who had been operated on for cancer of the bladder three weeks earlier. By the new administration's standards, he should have been discharged a week ago. The doctors would have to justify each day he remained hospitalized.

That evening, I leafed through his chart and read that Mr. Caruso had originally been admitted because he was urinating blood. The urologists diagnosed cancer of the bladder, removed the diseased organ a week later, and inserted a nephrostomy tube, which drained the urine directly from the kidneys. His patient care card noted he needed his penis irrigated and dressed twice a day. *Why?* I wondered.

I remembered hearing Karen tell me I'd see more penises during my Urology rotation than I'd probably see in my entire life. "The Urology Clinic is like a Gynecology Clinic with men in the stirrups."

Shortly after surgery, the surgeons diagnosed cancer of the penis, when the penile tissue began sloughing off. A week later, they had laterally amputated the bottom half of his penis. My skin crawled. Before leaving the ward, I peeked into his room and saw an old, emaciated, white-haired man—fast asleep. He snored through his toothless mouth. Aside from the snoring, he appeared lifeless.

The next morning I entered his room and introduced myself. "Mr. Caruso? I'm Miss Karels. I'll be taking care of you for the next few days, helping you with your bath and your dressings. Whatever you need, I'm here for you," I said, with a note of hesitancy in my voice. His dull eyes briefly met mine, and then he transferred his gaze to the window.

"It sounds like you've been through a tough few weeks," I continued, not quite sure what to say. "Do you want to talk about it?"

"What's there to talk about?" he barked. "You are changing my dressings, aren't you?"

"Yes, I am, whenever you're ready," I answered, even though I hoped I'd be spared that task. "Is there anything else you'd like to do first—a bath, a shave?" I asked hopefully.

"No, get the damn thing over with," he growled. "But do what *I* tell you to do. These doctors here don't know what the hell they're doing. They're good for nothing. They can all go to hell. Doctors, student doctors—this place is killing me. You hear me, it's killing me!"

Shocked, I said nothing for a moment.

"The doctors screwed up. They told me I had a tumor in my bladder and it would be a simple procedure to remove it. Then they got in there and whomever had the knife cut into the tumor and it spilled out all inside of me. And now the cancer cells spread down there, and it's rotting away and they cut away at it every day. Looks like a sliced dill pickle."

I was speechless. In a minute, he continued, "I'm sorry. You're just a kid. It's not your problem. And you shouldn't have to be put through this. I'm seventy years old, so it's not like I need the thing anymore, but by God, I'd rather be dead. Yes, I'd much rather be dead than put up with this every day."

A minute later, a team of surgeons paraded into the room, all wearing white coats. "Ahh, Mr. Caruso, I see you have a pretty young nurse to take care of you today," said the head urologist, a South American who smiled my way as he spoke. "That must cheer you up." Mr. Caruso just stared blank-faced at the team. "And what's *your* name?" the surgeon asked, looking my way.

"Miss Karels," I responded.

"Well, Miss Karels, we're going to show you how to change Mr. Caruso's dressing here. But first, we're going to debride it. You know what that means, don't you dear?"

*Of course I knew what debriding meant.* The surgeon pulled back Mr. Caruso's bedcovers, which had been draped over a cage-like device to prevent any unnecessary pressure on his penis. With all the interns, residents and med-students looking on wide-eyed, the cocky surgeon removed the gauze from the mutilated penis and lifted it up for all to see. The underside had a foul-smelling, slimy green surface. Mr. Caruso was right—his penis looked like a dill pickle, right down to the color. But instead of a crisp surface of a pickle, the surface resembled slimy cooked okra.

"Pseudomonas," murmured the surgeon. "Damn! Change the antibiotic to Ceclor. Give me the dressing kit. When did he last receive pain medication, Miss Karels?"

"About half an hour ago," I noted. "Morphine."

"That should do for this," he said, and he took a deep breath as he pulled on his glove. For the next ten minutes, we all stood horrified as the surgeon cut away the rotting penile tissue with a scalpel and scissors. Mr. Caruso just looked toward the window, gritting his false teeth, never meeting the eyes of the physicians.

"Watch carefully, dear," instructed the surgeon, "Every morning, you need to irrigate it with this antibiotic solution, for at least ten minutes. Then wrap it in Iodoform gauze, like this—but not too tight. You think you can handle that?" he asked, pulling off his gloves and glancing at his watch.

Emotionally worn out from just watching the procedure, I nodded silently. Then the surgeon gave Mr. Caruso a pat on the shoulder and said, “How many patients get a nurse like Miss Karels here, to grant their every wish? Can’t ask for much more in life, can we?” and with that, the group swiftly exited the room.

After taking a deep breath, I began my nursing care—I shaved him, bathed him, helped feed him and made his bed. He just stared out the window, refusing to talk. It was the same the next day, and the next.

Finally he opened up to me, saying, “You’re just a kid, younger than my granddaughter. Girls your age should be out having fun, going to college, attending parties, not taking care of sick people all day long. This is the world of the dead. You belong in the world of the living!” I thought of all the unmarried nurses in the hospital, nurses wed to their jobs--married to the County.

On Thursday, Mr. Caruso told me he would die soon because he no longer wanted to live. Before I left for the day, he asked if I would bring him bacon and eggs on Friday.

“I know I shouldn’t be eating bacon on Friday, but hopefully God will forgive me. I just can’t eat this shit that they give me anymore. Tasteless mush! A rat wouldn’t eat it!”

So on Friday morning, I asked for a plate ‘to go’ in the nurse’s cafeteria, with the specified fried eggs and bacon. They were a little cold when I got them to the ward, but Mr. Caruso wolfed them down.

“Thank you,” was all he said. “This is my last supper.”

Mr. Caruso died that evening. When I arrived on the ward Monday, a new man occupied his bed.

# ❖ 21 ❖

Rotating through the surgical wards was like a visit to an amusement park. Every ward was a different and exciting ride. But the Burn Unit was the ride from Hell, the ride that shook me upside down, rattled my bones and brain and left me feeling numb. And I was only there a week!

The Burn Unit was located on the fifth floor of the Pediatrics building. Before entering, we had to don sterile yellow gowns, shoe covers, cap, and mask. All visitors had to do the same.

Burn victims were flown in by helicopter from all over the midwest—farmers, stockbrokers, inner city children, suburban families—all shared the same close confines. We had studied burns before we visited the unit—the different degrees of burns, types of burns, treatments and rehabilitation. But the lectures hadn't prepared me for the shock of seeing newly burned patients. Most were on respirators and wrapped in gauze from head to toe. Even the recovering burn patients were shocking to see—those whose faces no longer resembled human beings and those undergoing skin grafting procedures. Those getting skin grafts were the lucky ones; many had no healthy skin left to graft.

My instructors showed us the hydrotherapy tanks—huge steel walk-in tubs that slowly rotated to a horizontal position. Then the tubs were filled with tepid water to soften the eschar, the tough, leathery substance that formed over third-degree burns. Once the eschar had softened, the nurse would scrub the eschar with a steel brush, similar to those used to scrub barbecue grills. If the eschar was too thick, the surgeon would cut it away with scissors and scalpel before the scrubbing.

"Scrubbing the eschar is the toughest job in the burn unit, physically and emotionally," our instructor told us. "Even so, it must be scrubbed off every day until the healthy skin underneath bleeds. The tissue underneath won't heal if the eschar's not removed. No pain medicine in the world that can take away that kind of pain. None of you will be doing the actual scrubbing."

I was assigned to a thirty-three year old lawyer from Lincolnwood. He and his family were having a family outing on a yacht. The yacht blew up and a flash fire followed. My patient had mild burns to the arms, legs and face. He was one of the more fortunate patients on the unit. They were most concerned about infection, for after the fire, he and his family jumped into the polluted Calumet River.

Lincolnwood, I knew, was one of Chicago's most affluent suburbs. I had never taken care of an affluent person before, other than to refill their coffee cups at the golf club. I felt as nervous as the first time I took a rectal temperature on that comatose man on Ward 28. Wearing my yellow paper suit, I entered his room. There I met Dan—attractive, blue-eyed, sandy-haired and burned. He had large dressings on both legs and arms. I had no idea what to do for him, besides talk.

"How did the accident happen?" I asked.

"My partner invited my family for a boating outing Sunday," he began, in a hoarse voice, his throat apparently still irritated from the smoke. "We motored down to Calumet Harbor and then the boat just blew up," he explained. "There was a flash fire, and we all jumped into the water. When the fire stopped, we climbed back on the boat and just stood in the showers until we were rescued. In retrospect, it was a stupid thing we did, jumping overboard. But at that moment, we just wanted to escape the fire."

"Is your family OK?" I asked, wondering where they were.

"We're all here," he replied. "My wife, my six-year old daughter, my baby son and my partner. I haven't seen much of them—we're all in different rooms. Truthfully, I haven't wanted to see them, after what happened yesterday. I had to wait in the hall while they scrubbed my six-year old daughter. I couldn't stand hearing her cry. I told them not to schedule us so close."

My wife's burns," he continued, "are to her chest, legs and arms—the areas that were exposed. The baby's burned on the legs. His chest was covered by the life preserver. The hardest thing for both of them is that she's still breastfeeding and he wants to grab her in the chest while he nurses. It's so frustrating for both of them. I'm not burned on my chest or upper legs because I wore a T-shirt and shorts. But my wife just had on a two-piece suit, as did my daughter. Their chests and legs were burned far worse than mine."

My instructor popped her head into the room to remind me that he was scheduled for scrubbing at 10. "Make sure he gets his pain medication." I gave him the Demerol and wheeled him to the scrub room.

After Dan entered the tank of water, it rotated to a horizontal position and filled with water. After Dan soaked for five minutes, the scrub nurses removed the dressings and began scrubbing the burned skin. It was torture just watching; I couldn't imagine what it felt like to be on the receiving end. After the scrub, the nurses reapplied the dressing.

The routine changed little for the rest of the week—breakfast, pain medications, soak and scrub and dressings. At the beginning of the week,

Dan seemed preoccupied with work. Even though he was burned, he was upset that he couldn't use a phone. He told me he'd missed an important court case that week, one that could make or break his career. But towards the end of the week, he became obsessed with the other patients he encountered on the unit, all in much worse condition than he. And he discussed his family.

"I never see them," he offered. "I spend my days in court and my evenings with my clients. On weekends I golf with my partners. If we socialize, it's at the country club, but even there, I spend most of my time with colleagues. Our wives talk amongst themselves, but about what I don't know, or care. We usually have a babysitter for the kids on weekends. This day trip on the yacht was an unusual one as a family. I've had more meaningful conversations with my wife this week than I've had all year. I'm starting to realize my priorities are pretty screwed up."

I was young, but I knew that it took a lifetime of reflection or a serious illness before most people acknowledged this truth. After a year at County, I would never take anything in my life for granted.

# ❖ 22 ❖

Four months after being laid off from Ward 35, when it became clear that students wouldn't be rehired, I began volunteering at a Mexican free clinic. I learned about it from a senior student, Carmella, who was active in the Chicago Student Nurse Association.

"Free clinics are grass-roots alternatives to the neighborhood Board of Health clinics, which are nightmares for a lot of people," she explained.

I had spent time at Fantus Clinic, adjacent to Cook County Hospital, during my surgical rotation. I recalled how the patients waited hours to be seen. They received morning or afternoon appointments without specific times. It wasn't even "first come, first served." Half the time, the Medical Records Department couldn't find the patient's charts, so the doctors working in the clinics that day didn't even know the patient's history and had to start from scratch each visit.

When patients received prescriptions for medications, they didn't get automatic refills, even for chronic conditions. So if patients missed an appointment, they could go days or weeks without the needed medication. Too many patients, frustrated with neighborhood clinics and the prevailing attitude that poor patients have all the time in the world to wait, preferred going to County Hospital's Emergency Room Walk-In Clinic when their chronic condition worsened.

Carmella continued, “It’s even worse if you don’t speak English. The Board of Health Clinics don’t treat illegals and don’t provide translators. So Mexican women often go through their entire pregnancy without prenatal care. Once the baby is born, they’re reluctant to bring them in for immunizations. And without translators, they’re not getting much-needed information on birth control. To protest, a few activist community groups have started these “free clinics” run by community members and volunteers. Drug companies donate medicines and hospitals donate supplies. A lot of County doctors volunteer in them.”

“How did *you* find out about them?” I asked.

“We had a guest speaker at the Student Nurse Association of Chicago meeting last fall who told us all about them,” she explained. “I’d volunteer myself, but I’m knee deep in wedding plans. And this OB-Gyne rotation is killing me!”

She gave me the phone number for the Benito Juarez Clinic on 18th Street and Racine, about ten blocks south of the medical center, in a predominantly Mexican neighborhood called Pilsen.

I called the next day, and made arrangements to be picked up the following Wednesday by a man named Alfredo. He told me he would be driving a red van. He told me he’d also be picking up a medical student and a physical therapy student from the University of Illinois.

I knew little about the Mexican community of Chicago except that they called themselves Chicanos. I knew a little Spanish, mostly words and phrases I’d learned from my mom when I was living in Iowa as a child. There, our house backed up to a cornfield and every August, trucks full of Mexican migrant workers arrived to pick the corn. Mom gave us lemonade and cookies to take to the workers and taught me how to say, ‘Buenas dias,’ ‘Como esta’ and ‘de nada.’

When I was fifteen, my family took a train to Mexico City and spent a week touring the city. I learned more Spanish words on that trip, mostly nouns and greetings. I was sorry I had taken four years of Latin in high school instead of Spanish. I asked one of my Hispanic classmates if she had heard about the clinic.

"It's at 18th and Racine?" she asked, looking incredulous. "You crazy or something? That's a dangerous neighborhood, full of gangs and immigration police. And since when did you learn Spanish?"

"I know a little," I assured her.

"How do you know these free clinics are legal?" she asked. "If they're not going to the Board of Health, they're probably treating illegal immigrants."

"The Student Nursing Association is encouraging students to volunteer, so they must be legit," I explained, not certain myself. "I think they get funding from both the County and the U of I." But I wasn't certain about even that. I really knew very little about them.

On Wednesday evening, I sat on the steps in front of the nursing school, scanning the street for a red van. Within minutes after the arranged time, a battered, red, graffiti-painted cargo van pulled up. The driver, a muscular, tattooed Mexican with a moustache and goatee, honked the horn and waved. He looked like a latter-day Pancho Villa, I thought.

"Are you Carol?" he yelled.

I nodded. He waved me to the back of the van.

"I'm Alfredo. The back door's open. Hop in." The van had no seats. I scrambled in, sitting on the floor next to two other students, a man and a woman. I felt relieved to not be alone.

A young Mexican wearing a brown beret and brown suede jacket with leather fringe, sat next to Alfredo in the front seat.

"This here's Lupe—my right hand man," said Alfredo, slapping the young man on the shoulder. "He's the leader of the Brown Berets. You'll get to know all of them once we get to the clinic."

With that, Lupe raised his right hand, in which he held what looked like a policeman's nightstick. I introduced myself to the man and woman in the back of the van. Bert the med student, and Alice the physical therapy student. The engine noise and the discomfort we experienced every time the van hit a pothole kept our conversation to a minimum. I hoped this clinic experience would provide the excitement and camaraderie I had gotten used to on Ward 35, but I had my doubts.

Alfredo talked non-stop on the way to the clinic. He told us how he helped start the clinic, how he was getting out the word to the community and his future plans.

"This spring, we're planning a community health day with screening for diabetes, high blood pressure and glaucoma. We're planning to have speakers on birth control, VD, drug problems, lead poisoning and whatever else you can think of. And dental checkups, vision and hearing tests. Maybe the three of you can help us plan it."

Before we had a chance to answer, the van came to an abrupt halt, Alfredo jumped out and opened the back doors.

"Welcome to Casa Atzlan, home of the Benito Juarez People's Health Center. Ever hear of Benito Juarez? He was the Mexican George Washington, the liberator of our people."

Alfredo pointed to an L-shaped brick building in front of us. "That's Benito Juarez," he said, pointing to a larger-than-life figure painted on the side of the clinic's wall—the highlight of a colorful mural. The words 'Viva la Raza' were painted above the mural.

"The people of our community painted that," he said, with obvious pride. "Just like they volunteer in this clinic. Nobody gets paid nothing. That goes for guys like Lupe here, who patrol our streets. Our people have to learn how to take care of themselves, to protect themselves, to be independent of the established gringo system."

Alfredo continued talking non-stop as he escorted us through the deserted playlot in front of the building. "During the day, this is a settlement house that provides day care, job training, family counseling, stuff like that. We rent space from them for the clinic."

Inside, teens like Lupe, all wearing brown berets, patrolled the hallways while swinging wooden sticks similar to the one Lupe had shown us in the van. I noticed they had a spiked metal ball on the end, attached to a string.

Alfredo acknowledged each gang member by saying "Hey my man, how's it going?" followed by the Brown Beret handclasp. Bert, Alice and I watched silently as Alfredo carried on with his followers, who clearly worshipped him.

He seemed quite a charismatic leader, giving pats on backs, hugs and thumbs up to all he met. Several had gathered around a huge Harley Davidson motorcycle parked just inside the building.

"When d'ya get it, Alfredo?" one asked.

"Like her? This beauty's my new wheels. I'm countin' on you guys to look after her real good when I'm busy in here, like she was your woman. Hear me?"

"Sure, Alfredo," they responded.

"Upstairs is the clinic," he told us. We ascended a narrow flight of stairs. "My guys are real special to me, and I don't get to spend a lot of time with them. I'm mostly on the streets recruiting, organizing and getting supplies. My official title is 'community outreach liaison.' I got a way of talking to doctors and administrators that makes 'em listen to me. They take me seriously." He led us into the office, where he introduced us to a Mexican man and his wife, Jorge and Rosa.

"Rosa and Jorge never miss a clinic," said Alfredo, patting Jorge on the back. "Don't know what I'd do without 'em. And they got seven kids too; the older ones help out sometimes. Rosa usually helps the doctor do exams on the women—for pregnancies and birth control. Jorge works in the pharmacy, with David here. He pointed to a slim white man with round, wire-rimmed glasses who had just entered the room. He looked like an intellectual Trotskyite.

"David lives right down the street, with Terrence," said Alfredo. "You'll meet him in a minute. They're our two full-time gringos. Everybody else is from *our* community."

"Wait a minute, Alfredo," protested David. "Terrence and I are as much a part of this community as anyone. Where'd Alfredo find the three of you?" Like three aliens from another planet, we introduced ourselves.

"Glad to have you," he muttered, scratching the stubble on his chin. "Hope you stay longer than the last bunch of volunteers. Most just come here for a walk on the wild side."

"David likes to kid around a lot," said Alfredo, who grabbed my arm and led me into the laboratory.

"This here's Terrence. He's in charge of the lab." A lanky man wearing a navy wool skullcap waved from behind the microscope he had been peering into. He had dark circles under his brown eyes and dark stubble on his face.

"Terrence is trying to get into medical school," whispered Alfredo. "He's really smart. Too quiet though."

I looked around the sparse lab, noticing a center table with a few urine-filled Dixie cups and a centrifuge. Other than that, the microscope seemed the only piece of equipment.

"What can you test for here?" I asked Alfredo.

"You'll have to ask Terrence that—I'm not the medical honcho here. I just get the equipment he asks for. We got an incubator and a small refrigerator promised—should be in next week some time. I know he draws blood, tests urine and does pregnancy tests. Ask him the rest."

One of the Brown Berets walked up to Alfredo, swinging his stick as he walked.

"Put that f--ing jucca stick away, Nicky," Alfredo growled. "You're gonna scare our new volunteers off if you keep swinging that thing. Come on. Let me show you the rest of the place," continued Alfredo, leading me into another bare room.

"This here's where we give baby shots. You told me you can give shots, right?" he asked, staring at me.

"I guess so," I responded. "I've never given them to babies before, but I'll learn."

"You'll also have to give Penicillin shots to anyone with VD," he noted. "We get a lot of that here."

A serious-looking doctor wearing a denim work shirt tucked into his well-worn jeans entered the room. "Here's Doc Elton," beamed Alfredo.

"Doc, this here's Bert, Alice and Carol. They're our new volunteers."

That first night at the clinic, we mostly observed. Bert helped Terrence in the lab; Alice helped David in the pharmacy. I assisted Rosalinda, an Hispanic RN, in the vaccination room. I took care of the paperwork and held the fifty-plus babies down while she injected vaccines.

The mothers all looked exhausted and seemed desperate for information. I listened carefully to the questions she delivered in Spanish and the rapid answers they elicited. I understood very little. I wondered if I could truly make a difference there when I couldn't speak the language.

"What are they asking you?" I asked Rosalinda, when things calmed down a bit.

"They ask about vaccines. I tell them what side effects to look for, and when to return for a follow-up visit," she explained. "But most ask me about birth control—what they can use that their husbands won't know about. Having big families is very important to Mexican men—a sign of virility and machismo. Last week, we had a woman in here, not yet thirty, with eight kids, the youngest just five months old. She came in for a pregnancy test, and it was positive. When I told her, she began sobbing. She had never used birth control. Nobody ever thinks about the quality of life for these mothers and their children."

"What do you recommend to them?" I asked.

"The birth control pill is the *only* option they can keep secret from their husbands."

The Benito Juarez Clinic was a far cry from Ward 35. It wasn't a highly charged environment where lives were being saved in heroic ways every evening. But, I thought, nursing wasn't just about saving lives; it could also be improving lives. Armed with the right information, perhaps we could help improve the lives of these women and children. I decided to give the clinic a try.

# ❖ 23 ❖

The next morning, Carmella joined me for breakfast in the cafeteria. "So how was the clinic?" she asked. I told her about Alfredo, the Brown Berets, David and Terrence. And I told her about the planned Community Health Day.

"Carol, that's a perfect opportunity to get student nurses involved," Carmella said excitedly. "We have to get the word out about this. Come with me to the Student Nurse's Association meeting next week, and I'll make sure you get on the agenda."

"Carmella, I've only been to the clinic once," I protested. "What can I possibly say that will make a difference?"

"Just tell them about the Community Health Day," she said. "Ask for volunteers. Tell them about your first night at the clinic. Tell them what you just told me."

The following week, a carful of County students attended the meeting at a small, private hospital on the north side. I spoke for ten minutes about the clinic to the packed room, and then passed around a sign-in sheet for the health fair after a number of students expressed interest in helping.

After I spoke, the president of the organization announced that elections for the next year were being held that evening, and asked for nominations for officers.

"I'm going to nominate *you*, Carol," said Carmella. "Cook County School of Nursing should have representation on the executive board."

"*Are you crazy*?" I responded. "I don't have time to get involved with this." I'd never run for anything before.

"You'll be great," she said. "Think of all the good you could do mobilizing student nurses to be community activists. Just redirect all that energy you put on Ward 35 to this."

"I really don't want to do this," I replied, apparently not convincingly enough, for by the time we left, I had been elected vice-president of the Chicago Chapter of the Student Nurse Association of Illinois. I shook hands with the other new officers—two white men in their thirties and a fifty-something black woman, all attending three-year hospital nursing programs on the north side. Jerome, Len, Bea—and me.

Bea was married with six grown children. I was still a teenager. We were a most unique executive board! Jerome assured me that all I'd have to do, as VP, was to find avenues for student nurses to get involved in community health activities. He'd take care of planning the meetings and doing all the administrative work.

I returned to the clinic the following week and presented the list of student nurses who had signed up to volunteer for the health fair to Jorge. Bert had arranged for the U of I Medical School Student Council to act as a co-sponsor for the event. Bert gave Jorge a list of med students who volunteered to help with the screenings.

In the subsequent weeks at the clinic, I filled in wherever needed, helping the doctors conduct physicals or helping Terrence in the lab. Occasionally David asked me to help him in the pharmacy, to discard expired medicine, sort donated medicine or dispense medicine. If the volunteer nurse didn't show up, I gave vaccines to babies.

When the clinic was over, around 10 p.m., Bert, Alice and I usually joined David, Terrence, Jorge and the volunteer doctors at the neighborhood bar, La Ponderosa. There we discussed plans for the upcoming health fair.

"Do you think you could get pamphlets, Carolina?" asked Jorge. "We need them in Spanish, of course—on birth control, VD, prenatal care, diabetes, high blood pressure and nutrition."

Bert offered to oversee the glaucoma, high blood pressure and diabetes screening booths. And Alice offered to find a local supermarket to donate fresh fruit and to find a source for free toothbrushes and dental hygiene brochures.

For the next month, I juggled nursing school and the health fair. I managed to obtain thousands of pamphlets—from drug companies, hospitals and infant formula manufacturers—all in Spanish.

The most unusual were the venereal disease comic books. These came from the Chicago Board of Health, whose representative told me the immigrant Mexican men would read comic books but not health pamphlets. These comic books were filled with sexual situations where the man always used a condom.

I thought of what Rosalinda had told me earlier, about how Mexican men didn't want their wives to use any form of birth control. I wondered what difference a comic book could make in their attitudes about sex.

The Health Fair was a great success with plenty of food, music and education. The workshops were standing room only. And the pamphlets and comic books disappeared quickly. Taking in the scene, I thought of the pioneer social worker Jane Addams, who founded Hull House. Casa Atzlan was a modern-day Hull House that served a new wave of immigrants. I wondered if the social work students at the U of I, just eight blocks away, even knew this place existed.

## ❖ 24 ❖

I often took the train home on summer weekends. There, I enjoyed the simple act of pulling weeds from my father's huge organic garden and eating the immense salads my mother would prepare. I enjoyed sitting on the back porch in the morning, watching the wild kittens frolic in the backyard, listening to the warble of the meadowlarks and eating freshly picked tomatoes and corn.

One weekend, I ran into a friend from high school at the local pizzeria. She told me she was on summer break. She too was studying nursing—at a four year college.

"Summer break?" I asked, incredulous. "It's only May!"

"We just got out last week," she said. "We start early, the week before Labor Day. It gives me a chance to make money during the summer and hang out with friends."

*Hang out*. I had forgotten what the word meant. Being on the trimester system of sixteen weeks on and a week off, year-round, was an unforgiving schedule at Cook County School of Nursing. We were immersed in nursing and oblivious to the outside world.

More than ever, I resented students in 2 and 4-year degree programs who had their summers off. I now realized that graduates of hospital-based training programs were getting the short end of the stick. We attended school the same amount of time as the students in university programs, yet to get our bachelor degree in nursing, we'd have to attend another two years of school after graduation. The whole nursing educational system seemed inconsistent. You could take nursing boards and, if you passed, become an RN after two, three *or* four years of training.

In response to her inquiry about what *I* was doing for the summer, I said, "Sixteen weeks of Pediatrics—without air-conditioning."

"No air-conditioning? What kind of hospital doesn't have air-conditioning?"

"My hospital," I replied. "Cook County." I didn't function well in heat. And Chicago's summers were brutally hot. I was sick of my hot, tiny room and the sweltering wards. I felt so isolated from the rest of the world. I didn't watch television or read newspapers and rarely listened to the radio. I was starting to feel trapped in County's tentacles.

We only ventured outside the Medical Center to attend college classes downtown at Loop College. But we never lingered in the city. We always rushed back to our hot little rooms to do never-ending homework—care plans and research reports.

Sitting in my room, I tried to imagine what it must have been like to be a 19th century immigrant woman with several children living in a room not much bigger than my own. No plumbing, no running water, no ventilation and no money. Just hope. And then I thought of modern day city dwellers: pregnant single mothers living in the high-rise projects, coping with too many children with no safe place to play. Thugs in the elevator, drug pushers in the hallways, broken glass and used needles on the playlots, and hostile gang members lurking on the streets. Life in the inner city, for most, was a miserable ordeal in the 1970's.

I was beginning to feel claustrophobic in the medical center. It was like a giant fortress and we were like cloistered nuns. I wanted out. I didn't care if the surrounding neighborhood was dangerous. I felt like I was going crazy. I prayed for an escape.

My prayers were answered when Karen and her classmate Rita asked if I would like to housesit their apartment on nearby Bowler Street that summer. They were both planning to attend Carmella's wedding in Europe after they graduated, then travel around for the rest of the summer before starting work.

Bowler Street was three blocks west of the nursing school, a tattered remnant of the former Italian presence on the west side of the medical center. Somehow, Bowler Street and the few blocks adjacent to it had remained intact while surrounding streets were filled with burned-out buildings, glass and garbage-strewn lots, deserted storefronts and stolen auto parts shops.

A TB clinic and an Italian bakery marked the southern entrance of the one-block long diagonal street; a non-descript gas station that fronted a numbers shop marked the northern one. Forty dilapidated two-story row houses and half that number of mature maple trees lined the tiny one-way street.

I loved their apartment! It was filled with plants, cheap posters, candles, wind chimes, Indian woven wall hangings and peaceful music. A ghetto retreat! I never noticed that the paint was peeling from the staircase walls, that the beams on the back porch were rotting and that cockroaches ran across the kitchen floors. Nor did I notice that the backyard was strewn with broken cinder blocks and glass, and overgrown with tall weeds, or that the graffiti-filled fence separating it from the adjacent row houses had fallen down. And I hadn't noticed the rats that ran through the alley. To me, the place was heaven.

Karen and Rita were the only students who rented on the block. The other rowhouses were owned by elderly Italians who couldn't bear to leave the old neighborhood. Their children and grandchildren from the suburbs occasionally visited them, always trying to convince them to move to the suburbs.

My greatest pleasure that spring had been to sit with them on their stoop under the shade of an old tree, eating an Italian ice, while sniffing the cooking garlic that hung in the air.

I was ecstatic about the opportunity to spend the summer three blocks away from the nurse's residence. Karen insisted I take the hospital security car to and from the apartment after dark. I promised I'd take it, having heard too many stories about rapes in the medical center parking lots and robberies on the street. To me, getting out of the nurse's residence for the summer was like a vacation to a tropical island.

# ❖ 25 ❖

Our final year would be divided into sixteen weeks each of Obstetrics and Gynecology, Pediatrics, and Psychiatry, with a week off between each. After completing these, we'd each spend three weeks as a team leader or 'charge nurse' on a designated floor, learning nursing management.

We were divided into three groups. Most of the students in my group lived outside the nurse's residence. Four were LPNs who recently joined our class. They were older, had children and were working to support their families while attending nursing school. Two were men, Matt and Aaron. Only three in my group still lived in the nurse's residence—Elsie, Sheryl and Shavonne.

Matt had a degree in Sociology and had spent time in the Peace Corps. He wore his thick, brown hair to his shoulder and sported a thick, bushy moustache. He was engaged to a Pediatric nurse and lived with her on the north side.

Aaron was married and had a degree in Chemistry. He looked like a blonde Sigmund Freud, with piercing blue eyes, a pointy blonde beard and moustache. He constantly stroked his beard or twisted the ends of his moustache as he spoke. He was the one who had made that mean-spirited comment about my not paying attention and asking stupid questions in Anatomy class. I had long since forgiven him.

The seven-story Pediatrics building was on the east side of the medical center complex, a ten-minute walk through the tunnel. With the exception of the fifth floor, which was the Burn Unit, each floor was dedicated to a different age group or specialty. The first floor was the Pediatric Emergency Room, the second floor was for toddlers to teens, the third floor for premature infants, the fourth floor for children who had had surgery, the sixth floor for infants and the seventh floor was Pediatric Intensive Care.

Some floors had specialty wings. One wing was just for babies with diarrhea. Another wing was the boarder baby wing, filled with abandoned babies. Their parents never came to pick them up after they recuperated! The parents had deliberately given the wrong phone number or the wrong address! Some things were beyond my comprehension.

My group enjoyed our Pediatrics rotation. The staff was caring and included playroom instructors and tutors who spent much time with the children each day. Because we were only on wards in the morning, we never met the parents, as visiting hours began in the evenings and parents were never allowed to spend the night.

Most of the children we cared for had common disorders such as contagious diarrhea, failure to thrive syndrome, meningitis, asthma, the croup, lead poisoning, hernias and sickle cell anemia.

Abused children also filled the wards. They were often children born to children or to addicts. They were neglected children who, left alone in apartments, ingested poisons or fell from windows. They were children sexually abused by older children, their mother's boyfriends, and/or step-fathers. They were children who had been burned, both literally and physically.

My first day on the toddler ward, my instructor assigned me to an eight-month old boy with multiple skull fractures. Before walking into the room, I peeked through the window and noticed ten steel cribs lined up against the walls, each with a bare-chested, diapered toddler staring out through the bars of a crib, waiting for a mother, grandmother or anyone to reach out and pick them up, to take them out of their cribs.

As soon as I walked into the room, they all began howling, thrusting their little hands through the bars, huge tears rolling down their cheeks. It was the first thing in the morning, and they were all hungry and wet. I found the scene heartbreaking. I wanted to pick them all up and hold them, to wipe away their tears. This was my calling, I momentarily thought, to end the cries of the poor, needy children of the world.

I went to the crib to meet my assigned baby—the only baby who wasn't crying and reaching his hands out from the bars. The baby looked at me in fear as I approached, with an other-worldly look I'd never seen in a child. He was a tiny baby and looked far younger than eight months.

As I pulled down the bars of his crib to pick him up, he released a shrill, ear-piercing scream and arched his body away from me. I managed to pick him up, but he continued to scream, struggling as if a wild animal were devouring him.

While all the other students in the room now held contented babies—happy to be held, to have clean dry diapers, and to suck on fresh bottles of formula—mine didn't want anything to do with me. I felt a total failure my first day as a Pediatric nursing student.

After ten minutes of this frustration, an entourage of doctors appeared in the door and strode over to me, exacerbating my self-consciousness. A large-boned, middle-aged woman with a short salt-and-pepper hairdo introduced herself. Her gray lab coat indicated she was in charge, an attending doctor. She was the first female doctor I'd met in the hospital.

She took the shrieking baby from my shaking arms. "Shush,

shush, you'll be OK."

Noticing the mortified look on my face, she said, "You're not the reason he's crying—he's just been badly abused. Did you notice the cigarette burns on his arms and legs?" I hadn't. She pointed to several small, round, dark spots on his arms, legs and trunk.

"The mother and her boyfriend are addicts," she explained. "When the mother brought him to the Emergency Room, he was unconscious. She said he fell out of the crib. But when we did an X-ray of his skull, we found two skull fractures. So we did more X-rays and found several untreated yet healed fractures of his arms and legs."

"Infants don't get skull fractures from falling out of a crib," she continued. "They're practically indestructible. These fractures come from blunt trauma. His mother's in custody right now, as is her boyfriend. Her other kids are in foster homes. And we'll keep this little angel as long as we have to."

As she spoke, she stroked his face and hair. He had stopped crying, but the terrified look remained on his face. "It may take years before he regains trust in the human race—if ever."

The group of doctors moved on to discuss the next baby, a little girl who was being rocked by an elderly woman. The baby bounced on the woman's lap and pushed her stubby fingers into the woman's neatly pressed, long-sleeved white blouse.

"How's Lakeisha doing today, Mrs. Manley?" asked the woman doctor.

"Oh, my precious little girl is doing wonderful, doctor," she replied. "She gettin' fat on all this good County food." The old woman didn't seem to mind that Lakeisha was chewing on her collar and grabbing at the thin brown sweater that hung limply over her shoulders.

"Well, just two more lead shots and we can send her home.

You'll be happy about that, Lakeisha, won't you?" said the doctor to the toddler, who now rested comfortably on the old woman's lap, not understanding a word the doctor said.

"I sure will miss this little girl when she goes home," said Mrs. Manley. Until that moment, I had thought she might have been the little girl's grandmother. Then I noticed that several senior citizens had quietly appeared on the ward. They were all feeding babies. All spoke softly to the babies as they rocked and fed them. In one room, I noticed an elderly white man rocking two babies on his massive frame, one on each shoulder. The babies sucked their thumbs and clung to him as if he were their own grandpa.

"Who are all the old people in the rockers?" I asked my instructor.

"They're foster grandparents," she explained. "It's a great program. Senior citizens spend their day just holding and rocking the babies here. In exchange, they get free meals for the day in the nurse's residence, and free bus fare to and from the hospital. It's a win-win situation for the babies and the seniors." The contented looks on all of their faces confirmed her statement.

After feeding my baby and changing his diaper, I put him back in his crib and walked over to the old man, still rocking the now-sleeping babies. "How long have you been doing this?" I asked. He looked about eighty, had a full head of white hair, wore wire spectacles and reminded me of a retired Santa Claus.

"Going on ten years now, I guess," he said, chuckling. Many of his teeth were missing, and a few of the buttons on his shirt had popped off near his stomach. "I wish I could say twenty. I love these little babies like they're my own. I wouldn't miss a day, unless I was so sick I couldn't make it. But, they keep me healthy. And as long as I got my health, I'll be here for them. I'm sure my friends here would say the same," he added, pointing to the other foster grandparents in the room. "These babies give us life."

After a few days on the ward, I noticed a little boy about four years old running around. He wore a little gown, had a tracheotomy and couldn't talk well. I noticed he even had his own little bed in the middle of all the cribs. I wondered why he wasn't on a ward for older children.

"That's Gabriel," said my instructor. "He's lived on this ward since he was one. He accidentally ingested lye and it burned out his larynx. He needs frequent suctioning. His mother couldn't deal with it and never returned to pick him up. So he's lived here ever since. The nurses have unofficially adopted him. He's not on the census."

On the surgical floor, I cared for a mildly retarded twelve-year old girl. Three weeks earlier, she had surgery for scoliosis (curvature of the spine) and was in a body cast. I noticed her legs were swelling under the cast, and she complained the cast was too tight. I told the doctors on rounds, who confirmed my observation, but were baffled as to the cause.

When the resident suggested a pregnancy test, we all looked at him as if he were crazy. But the test was done, and amazingly, it turned out positive. When the social worker later asked my patient if she'd ever had sex, my patient said she didn't know what sex was. After an explanation, my patient looked horrified and denied it.

The surgeons sawed open the cast. "Now we have two patients to concern ourselves with," said the surgeon, "a young girl *and* a fetus exposed to prolonged radiation and anesthesia."

Every floor had a social worker, and I asked many questions of them, even though most seemed burned out. *What happens to these abused children? Why were they allowed to return to their homes? Were they placed in foster homes? Where did they go once they became wards of the state? Why are abusive parents free to have more children? Who spoke for the children in courts?* There didn't seem to be a great system, other than the overburdened and under-staffed Department of Children and Family Services, which allowed too many children to fall through the cracks, it seemed.

On the Pediatric floors, we took care of patients whose fate, in large part, depended on someone else—parents, grandparents, foster parents, strangers. The abused children were little lost souls, and County's Pediatric Hospital was, for many, an unscheduled vacation from the harsh reality of life.

## ❖ 26 ❖

In September, I reluctantly moved back into the Nurse's Residence, as Karen and Rita had returned from their trips abroad and had started work in the hospital. A new group of freshman students had arrived, filling the rooms of friends who had graduated a few months ago. They all seemed so excited, so eager, so innocent. Instead of the typical freshman orientation, Mrs. R made arrangements for the entire school to go on a weekend camping retreat in Wisconsin.

I really liked Mrs. R, who was an effervescent, no-nonsense woman in her early forties. I sat next to her on the bus, and we talked about everything. She told me my class was the first to get college credits from three colleges—Malcolm X, Loop and Northeastern.

"You're going to need those credits when you continue on for your degree," she said.

"But I don't want to get a degree in nursing," I told her. "Why isn't this enough? How better trained can those degree nurses be?"

"Truthfully, they're not," she admitted. "You all get far more experience on the wards, and come out much better prepared to handle the everyday realities of nursing. But the nursing profession is changing. They want to be viewed as professionals and not as skilled workers. I've been reading a lot about the changing face of nursing, and I can assure you that most hospitals are going to be looking for that degree if you want to advance in the profession."

*Advance to what?* I felt sure I'd never pursue my degree in nursing. Three years of nursing school was enough for me. If I was going to work as a nurse, it would be at the bedside, not as an administrator.

During that beautiful Indian Summer weekend, we went boating, hiking, swimming and fishing. Late Saturday afternoon, several of us went horseback riding. We encouraged Mrs. R to ride her first horse, and she finally gave in, laughingly saying, "What the heck. Life is short." Two camp helpers hoisted her 300-pound body onto the waiting horse.

"She's gentle," the workers assured her. About forty-five minutes into the outing, Mrs. R' 'gentle' horse bolted and reared. Mrs. R fell to the ground, unable to move. We all jumped off our horses and gathered around her, trying to see how badly injured she was.

"I'll be OK," she moaned, but the fact that she couldn't move without pain worried us. After a half-hour, she said she felt well enough to walk back to camp with our assistance. Back at camp, she asked to lie down on her cot.

"You should go to the hospital, Mrs. R."

"No, I'll be fine. Just some bruises. I don't want to ruin this weekend for all of you."

She remained on the cot, clearly in pain, until about midnight, when her husband arrived and whisked her off.

Mrs. R didn't show up to school on Monday, Tuesday or Wednesday. Nobody would tell us about her condition. Finally, on Thursday, we were told that Mrs. R had been admitted to the hospital on Sunday. She had been hemorrhaging from her liver. The surgeons did an exploratory laparotomy and found cancer cells in her bones, her lungs and her lymph glands.

Mrs. R never returned to Cook County School of Nursing. She

died of kidney failure a couple of weeks later, at the young age of 42. She left behind a husband and two children.

Several of my classmates attended her funeral services at a tiny Baptist Church on the South Side. We sat there silently, all feeling terrible.

At least Mrs. R spent her last moments with the students she cared about, in an environment of joy and fellowship that she sought so hard to achieve among the students of Cook County School of Nursing.

Life in the nurse's residence seemed more depressing than ever. I was chatting with a classmate named Martha, who was telling me about the Psychiatry rotation, when my phone rang. It was Karen.

"Carol, I've got great news!" she said. "The family living downstairs is moving out next week. If you want the place, I'll tell the landlord to hold it for you. The rent's $80 a month."

An apartment of my own! I couldn't believe it. I dreaded moving back into the nurse's residence after Karen had returned. I felt like a pet mouse having to return to the cage after running around the house.

"Tell him to hold it," I excitedly told her. After hanging up, I shared the information with Martha.

"How much is the rent?" Martha asked.

"Eighty dollars a month," I answered.

"How can you afford that?" she asked.

"I'll get a job," I replied. "At the U of I."

"Want a roommate?" she asked. "Then you'll only have to pay $40."

The next day, after class, we stopped by to see the place. It was more like a hovel than an apartment. It had filthy wall-to-wall gold carpeting that the landlord, a macho young Italian in a too-small T-shirt, grudgingly agreed to have cleaned.

The apartment was one long space separated by two archways. The living room and the dining room had an arch between them, and a second arch separated the dining room from an enclosed back porch. It had a narrow kitchen with a buckling linoleum floor and ancient stained sink, a living room with a non-working fireplace, and a tiny, mildew-stained bathroom with a standup shower.

"I'll sleep in the dining room," offered Martha, "and you can have the back porch. We can put up a screen where the arch is."

"There's a bathtub in the cellar," noted the owner. "My father keeps the family wine kegs down there, too." We descended the long, narrow stairs, swiping cobwebs from our faces, to the musty basement. I noticed at least a dozen kegs of wine. The owner filled two-gallon jars with wine from one of the kegs. He pointed to the bathtub in the middle of the cellar, covered in dust, and noted we could use that in addition to the first floor shower. Martha and I hesitantly agreed to rent the unfurnished apartment.

The excitement I had felt earlier had transformed into dread. Daily life in the residence hall had been so easy—maid service, meals and security.

*Did I really need this apartment, the added expense, and the burden of furnishing, cleaning and maintaining it?* I had my toughest rotation coming up in January—Obstetrics. I was still involved with the free clinic. I was an officer in the Student Nurse Association. And now I'd have to start work somewhere to pay the rent.

I called my parents and told them of my plans. They were cautiously supportive. Then I told them about my Psychiatry rotation. Since County no longer had a Psychiatric facility, we affiliated at Madden Mental Health Center in suburban Maywood.

"How are you getting out to Madden?" asked Mom.

"I'll have to walk five blocks to the El train, take the El ten miles, then take a bus into Maywood," I said.

A week later, Dad called and said my birthday present was a used car—a navy blue Buick Special with 120,000 miles on it. *A car!* A car would get me to Madden Mental Health Center without walking those dangerous five blocks to the El every morning. And with a car, I could finally drive home instead of taking the train on Saturday mornings.

Shortly after the car arrived, Martha and I drove to the Goodwill store on Madison Street and bought a lamp, chair and kitchen table for $30. We drove past the low-income housing projects on Taylor Street to get an Italian beef sandwich at Al's. And we drove to Maria's Italian Ice stand on Halsted Street. That night, we drove up and down Lake Shore Drive, Chicago's Gold Coast, with the radio blasting. I had never felt so free.

## ❖ 27 ❖

I applied for a job at the University of Illinois Hospital, and days later, reported for duty to 7 East, a surgical floor. The head nurse ushered me into the staff lunchroom, where the end-of-shift report would soon begin, she said. I took a chair around the table, joining about fifteen predominantly white nurses, student assistants and nurses aides who had already poured their mugs of coffee. *I felt like an outsider.*

I sat through the interminable report, listening to the charge nurse describe each patient in detail—dressings, wounds, personality quirks, eating habits, the pre-op or post-op procedures that needed to be done. When report was finally over, the charge nurse handed me my assignment—a room with five men.

Entering the corridor, I noticed lights were blinking above every room. Call lights, I presumed. We didn't have them at County. Instead of wards, the U of I had rooms with five beds. The rooms had a petition with two patients on one side and three on the other. Each room shared a bathroom consisting of one toilet and one shower with an adjoining room. Ten patients per bath versus twenty to forty patients per bath at County, depending on the ward. Like County, patients could watch TV in the lounge.

I also noticed the patient population was more diverse than County's. At County, the patients were primarily inner city blacks. Since the U of I was a state hospital, patients came from all over, not just the inner city. Unlike County, the U of I also had Spanish translators on staff, so much of the Mexican community sought health care there.

It didn't take long for me to recognize the drawbacks of a forced melting pot in a hospital room. The men to whom I had been assigned could *not* get along. They included a Mexican plumber in his sixties who'd just had his prostate removed; a downstate farmer who'd had a cardiac bypass a week earlier; a black transsexual scheduled for a sex change operation; a professor from the University of Illinois Champaign campus who had cancer of the esophagus; and a young prisoner with skin grafts on his ulcerated leg, on strict bedrest.

The prisoner wanted to smoke in bed but couldn't because the professor required continuous oxygen. Not one to follow rules, he'd pull his curtain around him and sneak a cigarette.

Smelling the smoke, the professor's wife would immediately turn on the call light or run into the hall to tell us. She wouldn't talk directly to the prisoner, even though he was in the next bed. To make matters worse, the prisoner monopolized the one shared phone in the room. He also had a female visitor behind his closed curtain. His guard seemed oblivious, absorbed in his *Jet* magazine.

The plumber was angry and depressed over his protracted incontinence. He'd been operated on two weeks ago and every time they took his urinary catheter out, he couldn't control his urinary flow. "They promised they could take this tube out after a week, that I'd be urinating on my own," he muttered. "It's been two weeks now. I can't miss any more work, yet I can't go to work with *this* in me."

The transsexual, whose bed was between the farmer and the plumber, wore a sexy purple negligee, a curly black wig and gold slippers. He seemed contented just gazing at himself in the mirror all evening, applying and reapplying his makeup and brushing his wig. I wondered if he did it just to annoy his roommates.

The farmer had recovered well from his bypass surgery but had developed an infection along the leg incision, which required another round of intravenous antibiotics. He had been requesting a transfer out of the room for the past two days. He refused to open the curtain that separated his bed from the transsexual's.

The prisoner was monopolizing the phone which prompted the farmer to yell, "Are you ever going to get off that damn phone?"

"Be cool, man," the prisoner yelled back. "You don't want another heart attack, do you?"

The irate farmer, once he heard the receiver go down, grabbed the phone and dialed his wife, who had been staying at the Holiday Inn in Greektown, about eight blocks away.

"This place is a nut house!" he yelled over the phone. "I'm stuck in this room with a murderer and a fairy. I'm the prisoner here! Bring my stuff. We're leaving tonight."

I told the charge nurse about the imminent revolution in my room. I suggested we move the transsexual to a female room as he made the others uncomfortable.

"He's *still* a male," she responded. "So he has to be in a male room. The farmer isn't going anywhere with intravenous antibiotics. He's no fool. You'll just have to tell the guard to set limits on the prisoner's phone time." I felt like a babysitter for a highly dysfunctional family.

I laughed about it with my roommate later that night—the absurdity of the situation. The stories those men patients would all tell of their forced incarceration in that big city hospital.

## ❖ 28 ❖

My Buick Special came at a perfect time. How ironic that the B Building, right across the street from our school, used to be the psychiatric facility for the entire city, and now we had to commute to the suburbs for our training.

Of my group, only three still lived in the nurse's residence—Shavonne, Elsie and Sheryl. Having the only car, I offered to drive the small group to Madden Mental Health Center every day.

For the next sixteen weeks, my Buick Special transported the four of us down the Eisenhower Expressway to and from the Madden Mental Hospital, located in the integrated, middle-class, well-manicured suburb of Maywood.

The modern acute-care psychiatric facility provided a sharp contrast to the ancient Cook County Hospital. It consisted of a one-story sprawling main building linked to seven octagonal pavilions linked by tree-lined walkways and manicured lawns.

The patients slept, ate, played games and received therapy in the pavilions; the main building had an auditorium, staff cafeteria, staff offices and family therapy rooms. To the south stood the tall white buildings of Loyola Medical Center. To the north was a K-Mart mall. And directly across the street was a Baskin-Robbins ice cream store. In front of the Baskin-Robbins was a sign warning "Do Not Pick Up Hitchhikers."

Shavonne and I had been assigned to the same instructor, a blue-eyed blonde named Gwendolyn (we called our Psychiatric instructors by their first names) who wore her hair in a perfect French twist every day.

On our first day, Shavonne commented to Sheryl and me, "Now we're taking care of *your* people."

"What makes you think they're *our* people?" I asked. "Just because they're white?"

"No," she laughed. "Because they're all crazy!" I had been afraid of Shavonne in my first year of nursing school. Now she made me laugh all the time.

Over lunch, my classmates expressed interest in my patient, an eighteen-year old Czech immigrant whom the police found running naked through a city park at midnight.

"Why was he running naked through the park?" asked Aaron, looking at me intensely while he nervously bit his cuticles.

"Who knows?" I responded. "He only speaks Czech." I wasn't sure why I had been assigned to a patient who couldn't speak English, especially during a Psychiatry rotation, which was all about observation, communication and feedback.

My patient had a muscular athlete's body, tousled sandy hair and huge blue eyes. Every day he wore the same maroon plaid flannel shirt, beige corduroy slacks and leather work boots. All day long, he stared at the walls, paced up and down the halls and smoked one cigarette after another.

When forced to participate in group therapy, his feet paced in place and his powerful body rocked unselfconsciously in the chair. His Czech friends occasionally visited and left shaking their heads, after all attempts at meaningful conversation failed.

I called Mom later that night to tell her about him. "What do you do for these patients?" she asked.

"We talk to them, ask them questions, try to get them to open up about their feelings," I said, although I admitted it was difficult if the patient spoke no English. "And we play games like ping pong and checkers. But most of the time, they sit and smoke, talk to themselves or sleep in their beds."

"So, if he doesn't get better, will he just stay there forever?" Mom asked. Mom had grown up near Chicago State Mental Hospital on Irving Park Road and knew that once you were admitted there, you rarely left. And Elgin State Mental Hospital was just a few miles from our suburban home.

"Madden's an acute care facility, Mom," I explained, "not like Elgin State, where patients stay for life. Madden's more like a psychiatric hotel—you can either check yourself in or get committed short-term by your family. Once admitted, you've got about a month to get better. And if drugs and group therapy don't help, you get transferred to a long-term facility."

I told Mom about another patient in my pavilion who had problems communicating—an elderly woman named Shatzy, who wouldn't speak at all. Her family brought her in for self-induced muteness. Yet she seemed totally normal otherwise.

She wore a thread-bare dress, slippers and a shawl around her shoulder. Unlike most medicated patients, her eyes were clear and she wandered around the pavilion with a perpetual smile on her face, stopping now and then to put her arm around a patient and give them a sympathetic look. Occasionally, she'd stop in her tracks, close her eyes, reach her hands to the ceiling and take a deep breath, as if engaged in sun worship. She just wouldn't speak.

During group therapy sessions, the head nurse tried to bully her into speaking. "Stop these games, Shatzy," she'd say firmly. "We all know you can speak. You're wasting everybody's time." Shatzy just smiled, tilted her head and rested her hands in her lap, defying all. At times, watching these belligerent one-sided exchanges, I sympathized with Shatzy. Why must one speak? She seemed to communicate just fine with smiles and pats on the back.

And she threatened no one, unlike Matt's patient, a teenager who had threatened to kill his elderly parents with an iron skillet and kitchen knives on numerous occasions. The boy's rages were out of control and his parents were afraid to tell anybody. One night, seeing the parents huddled and crying on the lawn in their nightclothes, the neighbors called the cops. The police brought the son to Madden, where he was committed in full restraints.

"You know," said Matt, "we all have these urges to do away with our parents when we're teenagers. But how many of us have the guts to act on it? Somewhere along the line, these social controls got built in that keep us from actually doing it. But what is it that makes some people have no fear of acting out their impulses? My patient's a human time bomb. One week he's attending high school; the next week, he's here."

"The scary thing," I said, "is that there must be thousands like him walking the streets, filled with this erratic energy."

"What makes *me* nervous," said Aaron, "is that I'm starting to identify with my patients." Aaron's most recent patient was a twenty-seven year-old grad student admitted with acute psychosis.

"It's pretty scary," he said, pulling at the hairs on his blonde moustache as he spoke. "Could have been me. The guy just flipped a few weeks before he had to turn in his thesis."

"He's probably afraid of completion, or having to get a job," said Matt. "I can relate."

For Shavonne, the Madden experience was an eye-opener in many ways. The suburban setting, combined with the fact that most of the patients were middle-class or affluent whites, took some adjusting. She had been assigned to a young mother of three who was found wandering in the streets in only her nightclothes. When the police returned her to her house shortly after midnight, she acted as if she didn't recognize her husband and children. The police found no evidence of physical trauma or abuse. Immediately, they brought her to Madden and worked her up for amnesia and acute psychotic episode.

In the pavilion, she appeared out of sorts, confused and exhausted. She refused to groom herself, and when forced to come out of her room, she just sat with her legs crossed, her arms close to her chest, caressing her chin and cheeks with her one free hand, looking around the room expectantly, smiling timidly at no one. After taking care of her for several days and getting nowhere with her questions, Shavonne said to us at lunchtime, "I never seen so many fucked-up white people as I have here. Rich ones, too. Money don't seem to matter."

Neophyte nursing students often worry that they have every disease they read about in their medical textbooks. We were no exception, but we'd all gotten over it after a year. But in our Psychiatry rotation, we started worrying again. Even though we didn't have the stresses of the hospital, we all struggled with our sanity. The line between normal anxiety and full-blown psychosis seemed a little too fine.

To add to our fears, in the middle of our Psychiatry rotation, our future obstetrics instructor, considered one of the most respected and knowledgeable instructors in the school, had died suddenly, a rumored suicide. She taught class one day and was dead the next.

And two female students from the junior class had committed suicide by leaping off the top floor of the YMCA building on Rush Street. The incident had made the front page of all newspapers—"Cook County Nursing Students Plunge to Death in Lover's Leap."

And a graduate student who lived in the dorm had inexplicably gained 100 pounds and was found wandering the halls of the nursing school speaking incoherently. They too had seemed 'normal' just weeks earlier, like all the patients at Madden, who, according to their families, had been fine one week, then were whisked off to Madden in the middle of the night, suffering from acute mental breakdowns. *Could it happen to us?*

We all started wondering what it was that made someone cross the boundary from sanity to insanity. Where did you draw the line between normal worries and fears and full-blown panic and anxiety disorders? When did sadness become clinical depression? When did exuberance and energy turn into a manic disorder? And when did someone who expressed anger become a sociopath?

In the middle of the rotation, we confronted our teacher with our fears. She laughed.

"Everybody gets these thoughts in nursing school. You think you have every disease. You're just stressed out. It happens in your senior year."

"No," we insisted, "we need to have a major discussion on the difference between normal behavior and mental pathology before this rotation is over." So she arranged for us to speak with a psychiatric counselor at the facility--not part of our curriculum.

"How do you feel," he asked, "when you lose your wallet?" And he wrote down all the things we told him on the blackboard.

"Now, how do you feel when someone cuts you off in traffic, almost causing you to pull off the road? Or, how do you feel when you return home and find your front door open, after you were sure you locked it that morning?"

On and on the questions went. It all seemed so elementary, but all the feelings he wrote on the board—anxiety, sadness, panic, anger, rage, fear and helplessness—were symptoms listed in our textbooks for depression, psychosis, anxiety disorders, manic-depression and schizophrenia.

"These are the feelings and emotions of life," he explained, "just like love, elation, joy, ecstasy and passion. Expressing these latter feelings didn't make one a nymphomaniac, pervert, sociopath or manic depressive. But suppressing them might." We spent most of the day with him, earnestly discussing our concerns.

"If you think you have a mental problem," he laughed, "you probably don't. It's when you think you're finc, and everybody around you thinks you have a problem, that you have to start worrying." His counseling helped, a little.

## ❖ 29 ❖

Psychiatry had been a fairly easy rotation, but during that time I had taken on so many additional responsibilities that I thought I would have a nervous breakdown. I had the apartment, I had adopted a young German shepherd and two kittens from the animal shelter, I was involved with the Student Nurse Association, I was working three evenings a week at the U of I and I was still volunteering at the free clinic.

Halfway through Psychiatry, I received a letter from Jerome, the President of the Chicago Chapter of the Student Nurse Association, notifying me that he had resigned from his position a mere four months after taking office, which meant I was the new President! He wrote that he'd get in contact with me soon, and turn over all the paperwork. I telephoned him, and anxiously asked him why he had made that decision.

"I didn't have a choice, Carol," he said, sighing loudly. "I just don't have the time or the patience for this position, so I'm giving you the reins. And I don't have the time or money to attend those downstate meetings."

"What downstate meetings?" I asked.

"Surprise, surprise," he responded. "So many things they never tell you. The president of each district is expected to attend executive meetings in Springfield every six weeks. But the best part, Carol, is that they don't reimburse you for your expenses—not even transportation. It's part of the privilege of being President."

"I don't mind going to Springfield," I said, actually looking forward to an excuse to leave the medical center. "But I'm not really qualified to be president of this organization. And I don't have the time either! I just wanted to find nursing students to get involved in community health activities."

"Well," he said, "I thought I wanted to be President. I'm awfully sorry, but like I said in the letter, I'll mail you all the paperwork. And don't forget, the next meeting in Springfield is the third week in November. There's an Illinois Nurses Association Convention going on at the same time. I'm already registered so you can use my papers."

As soon as he hung up, I began thinking of ways to resign, however embarrassing, after the trip to Springfield. A few weeks later, while having breakfast in the cafeteria with my classmates, the new director of our school stopped by my table.

"Congratulations, Carol," she said. "I see you're the new President of the Chicago Chapter of SNAI. Would you mind addressing the new freshman class some afternoon this week—tell them about the organization, your goals, how they can get involved?"

I guiltily agreed to talk to the new students and share my 'enthusiasm' for the organization. I hastily prepared a presentation, and spoke to the new students about the free clinics and other community organizations in which they could get involved. I told them what a terrific place County was—how lucky they were to be part of the largest public hospital in the United States, how proud they should feel, being admitted to one of the most historic schools in the country.

As I spoke, I noticed this new class had men and women of all ages and races, not so unlike my class. But these students smiled, listened attentively, asked questions, and didn't segregate themselves by race, as my class had done initially.

I enjoyed speaking to them and answering their questions. To them, I was like Genelle was to me a few years back, a senior nursing student who knew it all! I felt like a hypocrite as I walked out, knowing I'd be resigning from the organization that I had so enthusiastically touted. But first I had to go to Springfield and represent the organization at the INA convention.

## ❖ 30 ❖

A week later, I departed by train for Springfield. Jerome hadn't made reservations for a motel, but assured me Springfield had hundreds of them. When I arrived, I phoned several listed in the Yellow Pages, but all were booked! I should have realized that thousands of nurses would be attending the convention. The state legislature was also in session.

Before giving up, I noticed the police station down the street. I recalled the time when my brother and I spent the night in a warm jail cell in Greencastle, Indiana, enroute to a spelunking weekend with the Sierra Club. I was thirteen; my brother eleven. Our parents' VW bus broke down in the town square just after midnight, and the police offered to put the two of us up in the jail, as it was vacant for the moment. My parents slept in the van. We slept well, and in the morning, the police gave us doughnuts and hot chocolate. It was fun.

Thinking the Springfield police might be in a similar position to help, I went in and explained my situation to the sergeant at the front desk. "I know this is an unusual request," I said nervously, "but I came down here for the INA convention without a confirmed motel reservation, and I can't find a room. Do you have a vacant jail cell? I'd be willing to pay."

"Let me talk to the chief about your unusual request," he laughed. I took a seat on the black vinyl couch in the waiting room and nervously began leafing through a magazine, as if waiting to be examined by a doctor. After a few moments, the chief appeared, a ruddy-faced middle-aged white man whose belly poured over his belt.

"Sarge tells me you're willing to pay to spend the night in a cell," he said. "We don't get offers like that too often." I explained how I'd spent the night in the cell in Greencastle, as a child, and that it wasn't that bad.

"I don't know much about Greencastle, Indiana," he said, "but our cells in Springfield stay occupied, and I doubt you'd want to spend more than a minute in them. Where you from?" he asked. He probably thought I was a country bumpkin who didn't know you had to make reservations.

"I'm a student at Cook County School of Nursing in Chicago, and I'm representing the Student Nurse's Association of Chicago at the convention here," I said.

"Why don't you have a seat again," he said. "I'll see what we can do to help since you've come all this way."

After about five minutes, he came out and told me he'd found a place for me to stay. It was a local motel just a few blocks down the street. He'd have a patrolman escort me there, he said. I thanked him profusely.

Ten minutes later, a young policeman strode into the waiting room and asked, "You the one waiting to go to the motel?" I nodded, and followed him to his squad car, climbing into the front seat. A metal grate separated me from the barking German shepherd in the back. I felt embarrassed as we drove to the hotel. He too chuckled about the fact that I had asked to sleep in a cell. "If you saw the kind of guys we have in our cells, you would never have made that request!"

I almost naively said, "I'm used to those kinds of guys. I take care of them all the time. I'm sure we'd get along." But I kept my mouth shut.

When we arrived at the motel, I noticed the 'No Vacancy' sign was lit. The policeman escorted me to the front desk and said, "Here's the girl the chief called you about." He turned to me and added, "You're all set. Have a good time at your meeting."

"Good evening," said the clerk, smiling as she handed me the key. "We have a beautiful room for you overlooking downtown Springfield."

I passed the restaurant on the way to the elevator, noticing that the evening special was prime rib with baked potato and salad for $5.99. Way out of my price range. $2.99 was the most I could spend for dinner.

I took the elevator to the top floor. After unlocking the door, I couldn't believe the room. It was a suite, with a king-size bed, a huge bathroom, a television, desk, sofa and a bar. *There must be some mistake,* I thought. *I can't afford this!*

I called down to the front desk and asked the rate.

"Oh, it's been taken care of," she said. "You didn't know?"

*"Are you sure?"* I asked.

"I'm sure," she responded. "Have a pleasant evening."

I didn't know what to think about this generous act on the part of the police chief. I rationalized that he probably had a daughter my age and wouldn't want her stranded in a strange town without a place to stay, asking if she could spend the night in a jail cell. He probably thought that if he didn't find a room for me, he'd get a call later saying they'd found me sleeping on a park bench.

Before I went out to get dinner, I wrote him a note of thanks on my Student Nurse Association letterhead, so at least he'd know I was telling the truth about who I was.

I woke up early to get to the convention, a day filled with

debates, seminars and guest speakers on the changing profession of nursing, the roles of nurse practitioners midwives, nurse anesthetists, physicians assistants, and topics such as labor relations, contracts and salaries. A huge delegation of nurses from Cook County Hospital attended. There had been talk of another nurse's strike at County, and I assumed these were seeking union support.

Most of the seminars related to specialty areas of nursing, so I attended one on "The Future of Nursing." And I didn't like what I heard. It was as Mrs. R had predicted before her death.

"It will be imperative for RNs to have their degrees within the next ten years," noted the speaker, an impeccably dressed and groomed, silver-haired woman who had a Doctorate Degree in Nursing.

"As a governing body," she continued, "the INA is charged with this responsibility—to mandate all RNs get bachelor's degrees, or else." *Or else what?*

She soon answered my unspoken question. "RNs without degrees will be performing tasks now relegated to LPNs and aides--basic bedside care. They won't be given positions of responsibility."

"And what if a diploma nurse was already in a management position?" someone asked. Many of the supervisors at County were County grads and didn't have degrees.

"We'll provide incentives for them to continue their education. If they don't, they may have to return to patient care positions."

I couldn't believe what I was hearing. If this were the case, why were hospital training schools, those who probably trained the most skilled and caring nurses, still allowed to operate? Were hospital-based nursing programs viewed as merely technical training schools?

I raised my hand and asked, "I attend Cook County School of Nursing and am the Acting President of the Chicago Chapter of SNAI. 80% of our members are enrolled in hospital training programs. Are you saying our schools are obsolete?"

"I'm sorry to say that those wonderful training schools will be closing in great numbers over the next few years," she answered. "I know that many of our country's finest nurses received training in these institutions, but they're just not designed to train the nurse of the future."

*The nurse of the future*. Just what was this nurse of the future? It seemed the nursing profession was uncomfortable with their image and confused about their future as a profession. Now that women had more career choices, perhaps they were worried that qualified candidates wouldn't select nursing unless the profession had more status and a degree attached. I heard all types of theories that day about the future of nursing. Hospital-trained nurses didn't have a rosy future in any of them, it seemed, unless they attended another two more years of college after graduation. As a senior student who was counting the months toward graduation, that didn't sit well with me.

As I boarded the train later that evening, my head filled with words for letters I intended to write, and would encourage other student nurses to write, before I resigned from the organization. As it was, it didn't make sense that you could take your state boards and become an RN after graduating from a 2-year community college program, a 3-year hospital program, or a 4-year BSN program.

There had to be an incentive to go the extra year or two for the BSN, and the INA was providing it. Get it or else. But did more book learning and less practical experience make a better nurse? I wondered what Florence Nightingale would have thought about the proposed reforms in the profession. After I thought about it, maybe she would have given her blessing. After all, she was the ultimate health care administrator.

# ❖ 31 ❖

I continued to volunteer at the Benito Juarez Free Clinic throughout my Psychiatry rotation. One cold winter evening, just after I'd finished cleaning up, Alfredo took me aside and asked if I would help him with a project on the third floor. I had never been to the third floor, but had always wondered what was up there. I trustingly followed him up the stairs.

Once upstairs, Alfredo led me into a back room. In the corner was a middle-aged, ashen-faced man on an air mattress. A sheet and blanket covered his body, naked from the waist up except for a bloodstained dressing covering his chest.

"What's going on here? Who is this man?"

"The immigration officials were trying to catch him last night," explained Alfredo, "and they shot him in the back as he ran down the street. He has a family he sends money to in Mexico, and luckily, *we* found him before the cops. So, *we're* taking care of him up here. Can you change his dressing?" Alfredo handed me a sterile new dressing and tape. With trembling hands, I removed the old dressing and noticed an exit hole under his arm.

"Alfredo! This man needs to be in a hospital! This is a major wound that could get infected easily. He can't stay here," I said, fearing this man might die at any minute and I'd be questioned for his death.

“Carolina, you have to!” he begged. “He’d rather die than be caught and returned to Mexico. Please, just change his dressing,” he begged. “That’s all I ask.”

“Why not have Elton come up and look at him,” I suggested. “He’s a doctor. He could assess this better than me.”

“He’s a *baby* doctor,” noted Alfredo, impatiently. “Anyhow, I don’t trust him. He might report that he’s here. If anyone finds out we’re taking care of him, they’ll close the clinic. It must remain a secret. Do you understand?”

I changed the dressings, feeling nauseous the entire time. When I returned downstairs, Bert was gone, as was most everybody else. As always, Bert had driven me to the clinic, so I had no way home.

“Don’t worry,” said Alfredo, “Bert’s probably over at La Ponderosa.”

I had my doubts. Bert and I had stopped going to La Ponderosa a few months earlier. Uneasily, I walked the two blocks to the bar with Alfredo, wondering how I would get home if Bert wasn’t there. Nobody else had a working car. I didn’t have money for a cab. And I certainly didn’t want to ride on the back of Alfredo’s motorcycle. Spending the night in this neighborhood was out of the question. We found Terrence and David sipping their beers in the back of the tavern, but no Bert. Alfredo explained my situation.

“Yeah, Bert looked all over for you,” said David. “Where were you, anyhow?” he asked. “We were all really worried.”

Alfredo responded, “She was sorting out leftover pamphlets from the community health fair upstairs.” Terrence offered to walk me to the El station and then accompany me on the El to the medical center.

“That’s a ten-block walk, Terrence,” I said, “Are you sure 18th Street is safe this time of night?” I recalled all the bars along that stretch and thought of rival gangs that patrolled the street.

"We don't have a choice," he said. "I wouldn't dream of sending you home alone," as he grabbed his coat and headed for the door.

"I'm really sorry to put you through this," I said, once we'd turned onto the tavern-lined street, lit up by flashing neon signs. Loud Mexican music blasted from the open tavern doors. Drunks in doorways yelled out, "Mamasita, besame (kiss me!)" as we walked past. After twenty minutes, we finally ascended the dark El platform. I sighed with relief when Terrence pointed out the bright light of an approaching train. When the train pulled to a stop in front of us, we quickly took seats next to the conductor.

We rode in silence on the train. The train pulled into the Medical Center stop ten minutes later, around midnight, when the evening personnel were getting off. By the time we reached the entrance to the nursing school, two blocks from the medical center station, I decided to spend the night in the nurse's residence rather than continue another three blocks to my apartment.

"Do you want something to eat in the cafeteria?" I asked Terrence. "It's open till one." He agreed, and we grabbed a tray, selecting dessert and tea. After a few moments, I broke my silence about the fugitive on the third floor.

"I wasn't really sorting pamphlets tonight. Alfredo asked me to change the dressing on a man who had been shot in the back. Alfredo swore me to secrecy, but if that man doesn't get to a hospital, he'll be dead. He told me he was an illegal immigrant escaping from the police."

"Immigration officials don't go around shooting people in the back," said Terrence.

"Promise you won't tell?" I begged. I pictured an angry Alfredo and his loyal gang of Brown Berets on my trail for snitching. Then I saw myself in a courtroom, trembling as the judge asked, "Well, did you or did you not change this illegal immigrant's dressing on the third floor of Casa Atzlan on the night of December 5, 1973?"

Terrence said, "The guy was probably involved in a drug deal gone sour. Thanks for telling me. Don't worry. Nobody will know you had anything to do with him."

I mentioned the incident to my roommate the next day and she just shook her head in disbelief. But Terrence later told me the patient had been taken to the U of I Hospital after he'd taken a turn for the worse. The incident had upset me and I felt used by Alfredo. That, combined with my demanding schedule of school and work, led to my decision to not return to the clinic.

When I told Alfredo, he acted distraught. "I was counting on you to help out at a community event we're planning next week. Please, can you help us one more time?"

I declined. I was too busy, I told him. On the morning after 'the event,' the headlines in the newspaper were "Riot Breaks Out in Pilsen. 36 Arrested. Cop cars torched." The photo under the headline showed two overturned police cars in flames. I bought the newspaper, and showed it to my roommate Martha. Alfredo was one of those arrested.

"Look at this!" I blurted. "Alfredo asked if I'd help at this so-called 'community event.' I can't believe what I'm reading! Two cops shot, cars overturned and set aflame. What could he have been thinking, asking me to help at this kind of thing?"

"Lucky you," said Martha, matter-of-factly. "He probably wanted you to nurse the wounded, like you did in the attic." She never thought much of the clinic. She had volunteered once or twice at my suggestion, but felt uncomfortable there with all the gang members hanging around. They never bothered me, and I actually liked most of them.

"I can't believe you've helped there as long as you have," said Martha.

## ❖ 32 ❖

I stopped volunteering at the clinic just in time. A week later, in my afternoon "Nursing and the Law" class, I learned that I was not legally covered for much of the work I had done at the clinic. When this realization hit me, I asked to speak privately with my instructor.

"Mr. McNamara, are you familiar with the free clinics in the city?" I asked.

"Can't say that I am," he responded curtly. "Why?"

"Well," I explained, "For over a year I've been volunteering at one every week, in the Mexican community. I do whatever has to be done—give baby shots, help in the lab, dispense medications..."

"What?!" he interrupted. "Dispense medications, give baby shots? Under whose direction?" he asked, staring angrily at me, as if I'd committed a crime.

"There are volunteer doctors there," I explained. "From all over the medical center. They write out prescriptions and I help fill them in the clinic pharmacy. Or, after examining a baby, they write out orders for vaccinations, which I give if there isn't a nurse there that night."

"And you've been doing this for a year?" he asked.

"A little over," I nodded nervously, thinking perhaps I shouldn't have shared this information with him.

"I'm not the only one, Mr. McNamara," I said. "I've helped

recruit lots of student nurses who volunteer there. It's a legal clinic under the auspices of County and the U of I. It's been around at least four years."

"And what if a baby has a reaction and subsequently dies from a vaccine you give?" he asked.

"What if a baby died from a vaccine I give as a student nurse in the hospital?" I asked back.

"At County, we have a billion dollar insurance policy for our students," he explained, his bloodshot cycs now bulging. "You are *completely* protected. Once you leave the confines of this hospital, young lady, you are entirely on your own." I bit my lip and thought about the seriousness of the situation.

He continued, "Carol, you're not even a registered nurse yet! Just because you know *how* to give shots, doesn't mean you can legally give them outside of the school. I can't believe you've been doing this. Not to mention dispensing medications. You have to be a licensed pharmacist to do that!" he explained, shaking his head. "What's with you?"

"But the guy who normally dispenses medicines there isn't a pharmacist," I said. "Why would they ask me to do those things, knowing they were putting *me* at risk?"

"Maybe they didn't know either," he said, softening his tone. "Knowing you, you probably let them take advantage of your willingness to do whatever they asked. You should have just helped in the lab, or with patient teaching. But never, never should you dispense drugs or give injections. Consider yourself lucky and get out while you're ahead. You've invested too much to lose it all now," he advised.

"Thanks, Mr. McNamara." I told him I had already notified the clinic that I was leaving, but I didn't say why.

A year later, I came across an article in the *Chicago Sun Times* on the clinic. After the incident with the police, the director of the settlement house, an Hispanic woman, threatened to evict the free clinic and the people who ran it, saying the space was needed for other programs.

I read that the clinic had lost its government funding because it failed to develop a close working relationship with Cook County Hospital. The government funds were supposed to pay for the salary of Alfredo and nine others.

I later learned, from the settlement house director, that Alfredo had pocketed most of the money. The clinic was now totally run by Alfredo and members of the Brown Berets. The chairman of Cook County Hospital's Family Practice Department, Dr. Jorge Prieto, offered to make the clinic the first family practice clinic in the county, bringing a massive infusion of money, staff and equipment. But the Brown Berets felt their independence would be compromised and turned down the offer.

"Those doctors have sold out to the medical power structure, which is out to destroy our clinic," Alfredo was quoted in the paper.

The director of the settlement house noted that her office had been broken into, a hangman's noose hung above her desk, her supplies stolen and windows broken. Trash had been dumped down stairwells and electrical sockets destroyed. She gave the clinic a deadline to leave and Alfredo responded, "We're not leaving. This is a very tense time."

## ❖ 33 ❖

Our final specialty was Obstetrics and Gynecology, one that County students traditionally excelled in on the national tests, largely due to the dedication and vast knowledge of the head instructor, Ms. Schultz. But Ms. Schultz had died suddenly a few months earlier. Our instructor would be Ms. Crabapple, Ms. Schultz' protégé.

Ms. Crabapple was the most frumpy, disheveled woman I'd ever seen. She seemed utterly unconcerned with her appearance. She wore a faded yellow, stained blouse under a shapeless, gray-plaid flannel dress. It was hard to tell where the floppy breasts ended and the flabby stomach began under her outfit.

Her dingy white lab coat was spotted with food stains. Instead of white nursing shoes, she wore black, fur-lined winter boots. Her unkempt afro looked like a much-used scouring pad with bits of lint scattered throughout. Like a clucking mother hen, she maneuvered us to a bed on the floor, one occupied by a new mother in her early twenties.

"Good morning, Miss," she said, fumbling to find the patient's name on her armband. "I'm Ms. Crabapple, the nursing instructor here and these are my senior students. We need your cooperation so these students can learn about post-partem care. Is that all right with you?" The patient, a young woman who looked exhausted after her night of labor, stared at us, wide-eyed and speechless, as Ms.

Crabapple gathered eight of us around the bed and drew the curtain.

"You just delivered last night, right?" she asked the patient, who nodded. Ms. Crabapple turned to us and asked, "You all know what lochia is, right? Who can tell me what lochia is."

Aaron volunteered, as usual. "The vaginal discharge after the baby is born."

"Very good, Mr. Hesse," she sang approvingly. "And just what should lochia look like the day after delivery? Anyone? Miss Fernandez?" she asked.

"Bright red?"

"Excellent!" With that, our instructor jerkily removed the top sheet and clumsily forced the woman's legs open, revealing a large pad affixed to her genitals. The patient seemed beside herself, but did not protest. Ms. Crabapple removed the blood-soaked pad from between the woman's legs and dangled it in front of our faces.

"You should be able to tell when she delivered just by looking at this pad," she said, seemingly out of touch with the feelings of the woman on the bed. "Like Miss Fernandez said, if it's bright red, she delivered recently. Each day, it fades more, until it finally turns yellow."

She turned to the patient and asked, "Have the nurses been massaging your fundus?" The patient shrugged in confusion. Ms. Crabapple began vigorously rubbing the woman's still large abdomen, kneading it like bread. The patient let out a cry of pain as she passed several large blood clots through her swollen, bruised, and stitched vagina, onto the bottom sheet.

"My, my," said Ms. Crabapple. "It looks like they haven't been." She then turned to us and explained, "For at least twenty-four hours after delivery, you have to massage the uterus to expel any leftover pieces of tissue and blood that may be clinging to the uterine wall. Otherwise, the patient could hemorrhage and die. It's painful. If it's not, you're not doing it right. Now I want you all to try it."

She grabbed each of our hands, and one at a time, led us in this exercise of uterine massage. "Um-*hum*," Ms. Crabapple chirped in her singsong voice after we each completed a turn. "That's the way. Now you." She grabbed the next student. "Remember, if it doesn't hurt, you're not doing effective massage."

When everybody had taken a turn, she announced, "It's time to take care of your own patients," and passed out assignments. "I want you to record the amount of lochia, make sure you massage the fundus and assist the mother with feeding her baby. At eleven, they have birth control classes in the sunroom. Make sure you go and answer any questions your patient might have." Then she turned to the patient and said, "Thank you, dear."

We all massaged our patient's fundi, as we had been instructed. We assisted with baths and prepared the mothers ready for feeding time. At ten, after all bedpans, food trays and washbasins had been put away, the newborns were wheeled out in their portable, plastic bassinets. There was no feeding on demand. Everything was on schedule.

Shavonne had been assigned to a woman who had had a stillborn baby. "It don't make no sense that they put her on the ward with all the new mothers," she said, as we walked through the tunnel. "I kept the curtain pulled all morning so she wouldn't have to watch them parade all them damn babies out to their mothers."

"Why did Ms. Crabapple assign you to *her* on our first day?" I asked. We hadn't even discussed how to deal with mothers of stillborns in class.

"She probably didn't know," replied Shavonne. We asked Ms. Crabapple about the stillborn protocol that afternoon. "Mothers of stillborns require the same care as other new mothers," she said, sounding defensive.

After learning everything and more about conditions on the post-partum floor, we spent time on the labor line, in the delivery room, in the nursery, and on the gynecology floor. We did not, however, spend time on the septic AB ward, filled with women who had had illegal abortions and had become infected as a consequence.

Ms. Crabapple drilled us until she felt we were experts on prenatal care, postpartum care, fetal monitoring, LaMaze breathing, delivering a baby, newborn care and birth control. We always accompanied the doctors and medical students on rounds. She gloated when her students knew answers to questions that medical students didn't. She trained us as if we were future midwives and she encouraged us all to consider that profession after graduation.

The labor line was as I remembered it from the day I had fainted—beds lined up against both walls filled with screaming, moaning, panting and praying women—young girls experiencing labor for the first time occupied stretchers next to women more than twice their age. Few patients utilized the LaMaze breathing exercises to ease their labor. Instead, they held their breath, grabbed the bars of their bed, released loud grunts, swore loudly, screamed at the top of their lungs, called to Jesus or silently closed their eyes and gritted their teeth.

I felt bad for the Spanish women, as the only Spanish words the staff used on the labor line were "cálmate" (calm down) and in the delivery room, "*puje*" (push) and "*tiene niño*" or "*tiene niña.*"

"I forgot all about this pain," moaned an older woman, already a grandmother. "This time I'm having my tubes tied for real. Soon as this baby comes out, I'm signing that paper."

After "mastering" the labor line, we moved to the delivery rooms. The labor nurses typically waited until the last minute to wheel a patient in, giving the delivery nurse just enough time to say,

"Slide onto the delivery table," "Put your feet in the stirrups," "You'll feel a cold sensation down here," or "You'll feel a stick down here." Within minutes after the delivery of the placenta, baby and mother were whisked away; the baby to the nursery and the mother to the postpartum unit. The room was then setup for another delivery.

We were supposed to work as a team for our first delivery. But my partner was nowhere to be found when they yelled out our delivery room number. Like the time when I had fainted, a woman had been rushed up from the emergency room. I had just finished practicing how to open the sterile delivery kit. I had laid out all the instruments, filling each basin with the required antiseptic.

When the patient was wheeled in screaming, I froze. Ms. Crabapple grabbed the kit and shrieked, "Prep her! *Now!*" That set me into motion, and like a robot whose batteries are being recharged, I helped get her legs into the stirrups, prepped her perineum with Betadine, unwrapped the sterile scissors and clamp, helped the doctor glove, and hung an IV drip as the doctor ordered, my legs wobbling like Jell-o the entire time.

When the shrieking baby emerged, I remembered to record the Apgar score after one minute, to inject the baby with Vitamin K, to instill drops into the baby's eyes to prevent gonorrhea, to attach the ID tags to both mother and baby, and to wrap the placenta in a plastic bag and place it in the freezer in the hall. It seemed like I held my breath the entire time. Ms. Crabapple was like a hovering basketball guard. Every time I looked over my shoulder, she was right there, arms flapping wildly, apparently making mental notes of everything I did.

I did well, she told me, and over the next few weeks, I assisted with thirteen deliveries.

At the end of the rotation, we were to follow a woman all the way through labor and delivery. I was assigned to a seventeen-year-old girl, Lonnette Fisher, one of the few white girls I'd seen on the labor line. She told me she and her husband had moved to Chicago from the south a year before. They were both very excited about having their first baby. I assumed they were from Appalachia.

After a five-hour labor, I followed her into the delivery room. When the baby emerged, he was very dark with a full head of nappy hair, *not what I expected.* Interracial marriages were still rare in the seventies and she never mentioned her husband was black.

As was County procedure, the doctor told her she had a boy, and the baby was whisked away to the incubator to get its shots and eye ointment without her even getting as much as a glance at it.

"Go tell my husband, please," she asked me. "He should be here by now." County didn't allow men in the delivery rooms or on the maternity ward. And they weren't allowed to see their baby until it was sent home. But they *could* wait outside the delivery room to hear news about the baby.

I thought about what I would say if the husband in the hallway wasn't black. "The good news is: Your wife just delivered a healthy baby boy. The bad news is: I don't think you're the father." I decided just to tell him he had a healthy baby boy, whatever color he was.

Just two men waited in the hall—both black. When I hesitantly asked, "Mr. Fisher?" the taller one stood up.

Although I performed well in the delivery room, others in my group apparently didn't perform up to Ms. Crabapple's standards. She shrieked, grabbed items out of their hands, slapped their wrists and generally humiliated them in front of staff and patients. And all of us did poorly on her tests, for no explainable reason. I had flunked the first test and gotten a D on the second. It was the only course I worried about incessantly because I couldn't get my grade up. For most of the rotation, my classmates and I were constantly threatened with the possibility of flunking out of nursing school.

"You think you're going to be nurses soon, but not unless you pass my course!" She seemed to delight in her threats to flunk us. In our Psychiatry rotation, we all thought we were going crazy. In our OB rotation, we watched our instructor have a meltdown, and like abused children who are at the mercy of their parents, we were her victims.

Our final trimester in nursing school was one full of anxiety and angst. I warned my parents that I might not graduate.

In the end, everyone in my group passed Obstetrics, getting B's or C's. Yet every one of us scored in the 99th percentile on the national OB-Gyn standardized test, the highest score possible. We felt vindicated by our high scores and reported Ms. Crabapple's behavior to the new Director. We didn't buy the explanation that Ms. Crabapple was under tremendous pressure to continue the high standards set by her predecessor. I might have chosen Labor and Delivery nursing, or even midwifery, as a career, had it not been for the mental anguish we suffered under her.

I was cooked after that obstetrics rotation. I couldn't imagine starting work right after graduation, as so many of my classmates were planning to do. I desperately needed a vacation after graduation and made plans to travel around the country for three months with my cousin Lisa.

## ❖ 34 ❖

Our final course was Nursing Management. We each had to function as a charge nurse on a ward for three weeks. That meant we'd be in charge of making assignments, making rounds with the doctors, and being on top of everything going on with every single patient. Mr. McNamara read each student's name and the ward they'd be assigned to. "Carol, you're assigned to Ward 21, the tuberculosis ward."

"Ward 21!" I groaned. *What had I done to deserve that in my final weeks?* My friends turned around in their seats and gave me sympathetic glances. We'd all heard rumors about the ward—Skid Row with clean sheets. I thought of all the miserable, drunk, rude, slovenly patients I had admitted on Ward 35 with the diagnosis 'Suspected TB' on their charts. I remembered their hacking coughs, and those globs of gray sputum that they expectorated into the bed, on the floor, against the wall and in your face. As I left the classroom, I looked defiantly at Mr. McNamara.

"Sorry." He shrugged. "Somebody's gotta do it. You never know—you might actually like it."

I dreaded spending the next three weeks behind a mask. But the day I reported to duty, no staff members wore masks. Nor did the patients. During report, I met the TB Team, headed by Dr. Wellington. He told me they had installed special lights that were just as effective.

Dr. Wellington reminded me more of a political candidate than a doctor. He wore expensive suits, he shook hands with patients and new staff, and he smilingly led his entourage of RNs, nutritionists, interns and social workers around the ward.

"Everybody's a part of his team," said the nurse's aide, "from the cleaning lady to the dietary workers. He don't leave out nobody."

For the next three weeks, Dr. Wellington made me an integral part of 'the team.' His enthusiasm was infectious and he restored my withering interest in County. Although he was clearly wealthy, he was sincerely interested in the downtrodden.

To my classmate's surprise, I couldn't stop talking about how much I enjoyed the TB ward. When Dr. Wellington asked if I'd consider joining the TB team after graduation, I was awestruck.

"But I'm going on vacation for three months," I stammered.

He frowned. I'm sure he expected me to say, "But for you, I won't go." But I didn't.

"Perhaps we can wait," he replied. "I'll talk to the members of the team."

Over lunch, I excitedly told Matt and Shavonne about his offer. "The TB Team?" asked Matt, incredulous. "Are you sure you're just not enamored with the man? Really, Carol. I'm sure the glamor will wear thin after a few weeks. If it wasn't for his personality, nobody would work there. And even *you* said he's only there for an hour a day, right?"

This was all true. Dr. Wellington spent most of his time at Michael Reese Hospital, where he was chairman of the Pulmonary Department.

"But it's a dream job," I said.

"Taking care of TB patients for eight hours a day is no dream job, Carol. The only thing worse is the detox floor. Don't commit yourself. Take your vacation and put it all into perspective."

As we spoke, the supervisor of Ward 35 approached our table. "Hi, Mrs. Lively. How's it going over there?"

"Same as always," she cackled. "Busy with a capital B. I thought for sure we'd hear from you by now. Every time I see you, you tell me how much you miss us. And here you are, graduating in a few weeks, and I haven't heard a peep from you. We need some new County grads to liven the place up."

"Aren't Miss Nixon and Miss Johnson still there?" I asked.

"Nah," she shook her head, "they left a long time ago, shortly after the layoffs. We have a bunch of Malcolm X grads up there now. And they're not bad."

"I'm taking off for three months. I'm not sure what I want to do when I get back, but Ward 35 is #1 right now," I lied. I always thought I'd work on Ward 35, but now I wasn't sure.

"Give me a call after you take your boards," she said. "I'll hold a place for you on the day shift."

## ❖ 35 ❖

Forty students graduated from Cook County School of Nursing in June 1974, from the initial 150. My class had been part of so many dramas in those three years: the untimely death of classmates and instructors, the death of one director and the resignations of two others, the firing and mass resignations of doctors, the layoffs, the nurse's strike, the constant threat to close the hospital during our three years, and the often absurd rules of the school.

My class didn't produce a yearbook in our senior year, the first class in history to have not done so. Nobody cared. But most of us did manage to get downtown and have our senior photos taken at a studio on Wabash Avenue for the class photo that would hang on the third floor. Just days before the graduation ceremony, Mr. McNamara chided me for having worn earrings in my graduation photo. "How many times did I tell your class to not wear jewelry for that photo? You and that damned Thalia ruined the whole picture. Not in fifty years has anyone worn earrings in that photo!"

And we did participate in the planning of our graduation ceremony. Our first choice for graduation speaker was the *Chicago Sun Times* newspaper columnist Mike Royko. He declined, saying he was a better writer than speaker. Our second choice, Jane Kennedy, a former nurse and anti-war activist who had spent time in jail with the Berrigan Brothers, accepted our invitation. I'm not sure how pleased the administration was with our choice but they didn't object.

In addition to my parents, several relatives from all over the midwest came. Misses Jones, the now ninety-year old volunteer, came. My nursing student friends who had graduated the year before came. And my California cousin Judy, a stewardess on a Chicago layover, came. I had sent her a letter during my OB rotation saying I didn't think I'd graduate. She didn't know what to expect when my parents invited her.

Before the ceremony, Mr. McNamara asked, "How do you pronounce your last name again? I always seem to get it wrong." I told him it rhymed with Charles.

Nonetheless, when it came time to read my name, he rhymed the first with the last, as he always did. He shook my hand and handed me my pin, a gold-plated one on which Florence Nightingale's image was engraved. A tiny diamond chip embedded in the pin depicted her famous light. I clasped it in my hand and returned to my seat. I couldn't believe this moment had finally come.

Later, when awards were announced, I learned I'd graduated with high honors, along with five others. Cousin Judy exclaimed, afterwards, "Hey Florence Nightingale. We all thought you weren't going to graduate and you got high honors! What happened between last month and today?"

Mom was radiant. Even though I'd had it with the place, nursing school was the perfect place to spend those high energy, high curious years. Nursing school was both an emotional and academic challenge, unlike any I'd had before or would have later.

Dad shook his head in disbelief. "I really never thought you'd stay more than a month." *Nor did I!*

The graduates and their families were all invited back to the nurse's residence for a reception—our last 'tea.' It was bittersweet. Most of my classmates had already made plans to stay on at County after graduation, and many planned to start work the week after graduation, as graduate nurses.

A few were leaving the area for good, returning to the states or countries they called home. And a small number planned to start work at private hospitals in the Chicago area.

My parents gave me a 'new' used car for graduation, one that could handle mountains better than my Buick Special. I sold the Buick to my roommate Martha, and gave her three months rent. The Monday after graduation, I headed for Washington D.C. with a duffel bag full of clothes, a two-man tent, a sleeping bag, $800, and my nursing review books. It would be the longest amount of time I'd spent away from the County, and my family, in three years. But I'd be back in three months to take my State Licensing Boards.

That summer, the summer of 1974, my cousin Lisa and I visited twenty-three states and four Canadian provinces. At eighteen, Lisa had never traveled far from her home state of Virginia and had never camped before. At twenty, I was a veteran camper, and my parents had already taken me to forty states in our VW bus. It had been three years since I'd camped, and it was the first time doing so without my parents.

We spent most of the summer exploring national parks. In the evenings, we attended ranger talks and learned all about the landforms, flora and fauna of the parks we were visiting. I made a mental note to go back to college and study Geology once I got back, just to better understand all the unusual things we'd seen. Just as County had woven me into its spell, the wilderness was weaving me into its own. I had left nursing far behind, or so I thought.

One night, as we sat around a campfire in a valley surrounded by mountains, I was shocked to see a car veer off the mountain road and roll down the steep banks. Lisa and I ran to the male campers nearest us and told them there had been an accident. I told them I was a graduate nurse. I jumped in the back of their pickup and we tore up the mountain, spitting gravel, guided by the upside down car's still lit headlights. They briefly stopped at the park entrance to tell the ranger to call for emergency help. The ranger followed us in his truck, bringing ropes, blankets, and a first aid kit. After our truck had gotten as close as it could to the car, we made the rest of the way on foot on the rocky, slippery slopes.

Inside the car was a semi-conscious woman who reeked of alcohol. The ranger recognized her as a local woman, and expressed surprise that she had survived the crash. I took her pulse, checked her pupils, and wrapped the blanket around her. Her face was bloody, but the rest of her body seemed intact. But there was no way any of us were going to move her until additional help arrived.

Soon, an ambulance did arrive and the emergency workers quickly scaled the slope, bringing a trauma board and neck brace. They deftly extracted her from the car, skillfully and gently placed her on the trauma board, and whisked her up the hill to the waiting ambulance. I was fascinated at how they administered emergency care in the wilderness, on the side of a mountain, in the dark. My adrenaline was pumping. The old familiar feelings of the hospital briefly came back. *I could be doing this, I thought.*

Until then, I'd assumed I'd return to Cook County Hospital when I got back. After witnessing the mountain rescue, however, I wasn't sure I wanted to return to County. I started fantasizing about being a National Parks nurse. After that, I visited the nurse's office in every national park and spoke with the nurses about their job responsibilities. Most had their own cabins and dispensed First Aid during the day. They told me they often went on helicopter rescues, treating injured hikers and mountain climbers for broken bones, dehydration, shock, frostbite, snakebite and internal injuries.

They all agreed that working as a National Parks nurse could be exciting and rewarding, but that you had to be independent and make many decisions, as there usually wasn't a doctor around. I especially enjoyed speaking with the nurse at Yellowstone. She socialized with the rangers, and invited us to go swimming in the Yellowstone River, at a secret place where the hot waters from the geysers intersected the cold river. She had a fireplace and potbelly stove in her cabin, alongside her single bed with red-checkered bedspread.

It seemed like heaven, to be immersed in the smell of pine needles and campfires. She gave me the phone number of where I could call for an application to become a National Park nurse. But she told me the prerequisite would be at least one year of Emergency Room experience as an RN.

Seeing my dejected look, she said, "Believe me, you don't want to come here just out of school. You have to make a lot of tough decisions on your own in these mountains," she warned. "It's a lot of fun but it can be very intense at times."

I wanted to tell her, "But I graduated from Cook County School of Nursing. It's the best." But I didn't. I knew there was a lot I hadn't seen. I hoped Ward 35 would qualify as Emergency Room experience, because right there and then, I made the decision to return there after this vacation.

I called Mom from Yellowstone in late July, and asked her to get an application for County. I had a sudden sense of urgency. In one year, I'd have the experience I'd need to return to the west, to the mountains, to my own cabin in Yellowstone, Yosemite or Glacier Park. I had a new sense of purpose. I visualized myself in khaki pants, a windbreaker and hiking boots, wearing a green nametag saying *Carol Karels, RN, Yellowstone National Park.*

In late August, Lisa and I were both ready to go home. Our last night, we camped in a barren KOA campground in Nebraska, the only tent in a field full of mobile trailers, surrounded by the smells of fresh mown grass and cow manure. I had loved the smells of the trip—the seashore, the mountains, the pine forests and the desert. Now, after traveling 11,000 miles, I was heading back to the smells of the County, *for one year.* I wrote a note to myself: "One year only."

## ❖ 36 ❖

True to her promise, Mrs. Lively held a position for me on Ward 35, on the 7-3 day shift. I took my Nursing Boards, purchased four white nursing uniforms, and returned to my apartment on Bowler Avenue.

The good news was that the hospital was crisis-free at the moment. It had recently passed accreditation and was attracting American interns again. Nurses made a good starting salary, $20,000, and received full benefits and four weeks vacation. As a result of this generous package, a larger number of non-County trained nurses were applying for jobs. In fact, three of the RNs on Ward 35's day shift were recent graduates of Malcolm X College's new 2-year nursing program.

Ward 35 was well-supplied and well-staffed. We still admitted the types of patients I had remembered when I was a student assistant—those with heart attacks, strokes, uncontrolled diabetes and high blood pressure, TB, drug overdoses and DT's.

The not-so-good news was that I was already regretting my return. I found everything dreary and depressing--the medical center, my apartment, my roommate, the neighborhood. *How had I spent the past three years there?*

My three months of freedom had released me from County's seductive grip. I missed the trees, the lakes, the fresh air, the stars and the big night sky. Worst of all, the day shift on Ward 35 was dead! We'd arrive at 7 a.m. There were typically four or five stable patients left over from the night shift waiting for beds to become available on the wards. New patients slowly trickled in from the Emergency Room during the day, but rush hour began *after* my shift ended.

Over time, I learned to appreciate the slower pace. I was able to spend more time assisting with histories and physicals, and learned much that I might not have had the pace been frantic. And I had more time to chat with the doctors, med students and patients.

One afternoon, I admitted an overdose—a hippie whose long stringy hair was matted with dried puke. Snot drained from his nose, tears dripped from his bloodshot eyes, and sweat beaded on his green forehead. He looked like a human in the process of morphing into a lizard. A well-dressed, well-kempt man accompanied him. I helped remove the patient's expensive leather jacket and cowboy boots. He was conscious, but barely, and couldn't answer my questions, so I directed them toward his companion.

The companion told me the patient was a musician in a rock band, and that he, the companion, was the band's manager. They had been performing in St. Louis the day before when the musician first got sick. At first they thought it was food poisoning, then they realized he'd taken some powerful drugs. His condition deteriorated throughout the day, as they rode the bus into Chicago, the manager told me. In my mind, I pictured a group of rowdy and disheveled rock musicians on the Greyhound bus, all looking on in disgust as this one puked in the latrine.

The doctor started an IV, inserted a naso-gastric tube and gave an injection of Narcan to reverse the effects of the drug. I continued to question the companion. "Has he taken drugs before? Do you know what he took? Do you know when he took them? Has he done intravenous drugs before?"

"Yes, no, no, yes," came the answers.

Then, between medical questions, I asked if they were a local band. The manager said no, they were on a national tour, and told me the name of the band. It didn't ring any bells.

"Cool," I responded, and continued asking medical questions. It was already late in the afternoon and several new patients had been admitted while I was taking his history. Ward 35 was packed with interns, residents and med students, writing notes at the desk.

I walked up to a group of medical students and asked, "Have any of you ever heard of a rock group called (…)?"

"Has anyone *not heard of* ..?!," replied one.

"Are they really popular?" I asked.

"Geez, Carol," said one. "They're performing for three nights at the Chicago Stadium this weekend. The concert's been sold out for months!" He began singing a song I recognized and knew was on the top of the charts.

"Oh, God. They sing *that* song?" I felt so embarrassed. They were clearly a famous rock group and I'd never heard of them. Although I had been a music reporter for the local paper when I was in high school, I hadn't kept up with the white progressive rock music scene. I recognized songs, but couldn't tell you if they were performed by Fleetwood Mac, Crosby, Stills and Nash, the Allman Brothers, the Dooby Brothers, or Acrosmith. But I *could* differentiate the music of black musicians such as Al Green, Isaac Hayes, Marvin Gaye, Billy Paul, and Harold Melvin and the Blue Notes. Whenever there was a dance at Karl Meyer Hall, the deejay only played soul music.

"Well, one of the musicians *won't* one be performing tonight," I said. "He's over in Room 3. An OD."

"You're joking, aren't you?" said one. I shook my head. They all raced over to peak through the curtain. A few minutes later, I returned to the room and asked the manager, “Where are you staying?”

“The Continental Plaza Hotel, on Michigan Avenue,” he replied.

“Just out of curiosity, why did you bring him *here*, to the County Hospital, and not Wesley-Passavant?” I asked. Wesley-Passavant was a private hospital affiliated with Northwestern University Medical School where most of Chicago’s rich and famous sought treatment. It was just blocks from their hotel.

“We figured nobody would recognize him here,” the manager replied. “At any private hospital, word would get out to the press, and then his fans would be sneaking him drugs again.”

They came to the right place and had the perfect clueless nurse.

# ❖ 37 ❖

Two months after returning to Chicago, I moved out of my apartment on Bowler Street into a basement apartment on north Western Avenue, forty blocks due north of the medical center. It was the same apartment my parents had lived in when they first married, and where I spent my first three years as a child.

The basement apartment had been unoccupied since my parents had been evicted seventeen years before. The same stove, sink, cabinets, bathroom fixtures and closet curtains my parents had used still remained. Even the mural my father had painted on the living room wall, the backdrop for my childhood Christmas photos, was still there. Now, however, everything was covered in cobwebs and dust.

It was no coincidence that I moved into that apartment. Earlier in the summer, my parents received a letter from their former landlord, an old Swedish man named Arndt. It was the first they'd heard from him since he evicted them in 1956, but he somehow tracked them down. In his letter, he apologized for kicking them out. He admitted he acted in haste after my father's rowdy Boy Scout troop camped out in the backyard. Arndt wrote that he had terminal cancer and wanted to will the house to my parents, saying they were the truest friends he'd ever had in America.

He wrote to them that his first wife had died, and that his second one had been nothing but trouble. She tried to kill him several times, he alleged, by poisoning his food. He didn't want her to inherit the whole house. He wanted my parents to have the other half.

He died in September, after changing his will and meeting with my parents. So, when I told my parents I wanted to move out of the Bowler apartment, they suggested I move into their old basement apartment for a while, rent free, until the house was sold. And so I did. I cleared the cobwebs, scrubbed the floors, dusted the surfaces, and moved in. I lived downstairs and the wicked widow Anna lived upstairs. I woke every morning at 5:30, and drove my car south on Western Avenue, past forty blocks of burned-out buildings, to the medical center, to start work at 7.

After moving, I called my friend Matt, who now worked at Children's Memorial Hospital on the north side. I met him and his new wife Laura for dinner a few weeks later. We talked about my trip, and the differences between County and Children's Hospitals. I told him Ward 35 on the day shift had been slow at first, but was getting busier.

He asked if I had met a doctor named Luke."I spent some time in the Peace Corps with him," he said, "and he just started his internship at County. If you see him, tell him I said hello."

I promised I would.

Later that week, I met Luke on his first night on-call and shared Matt's message.

"It's been a while since I've seen him," said Luke. "When are you planning to visit him again? Maybe we can go together." I called Matt the next morning and we set up a date for the following Sunday.

Luke didn't own a car so I picked him up. There was a blizzard that day and it was slow going in the snow, so we had time to get to know each other. Luke told me he had been visiting the sick at County since he was a teenager, as part of his community service commitment at his Catholic high school. He'd worked his way through college, took time off to join the Peace Corps in Latin America, and later went to medical school.

I told him about Mom and how she delivered coats and cookies to the County. I told him I'd worked as a busgirl at a golf club when I was a teenager. He told me he'd worked as a golf caddy when he was a teenager, also at a local golf club.

I got to know him even better at Matt's, as each brought the other up to date on their individual lives. It was a night of good food and lots of laughter. There was none of the tension usually associated with first dates. I hoped to see him again.

"Are you going out again?" asked Elsie, who had become my closest friend. She was impressed that I had 'gotten a date' with him five minutes after meeting him. "Every nurse in Pediatrics was trying to go out with him. What did you do?"

"It wasn't really a date," I said. "We just went to visit Matt and they caught up on the past several years."

A few weeks later, he asked me out again, to go ice skating with a group of his friends, several of whom he served with in the Peace Corps. His friends were all social activists. I also learned he lived in an informal commune with several of them in Pilsen. Although they all passionately discussed Chicago politics and social issues, they had tremendous senses of humor, and much of the night was spent laughing.

After skating, we all headed for their shared house, just blocks from the Benito Juarez Clinic. As we passed the clinic, I told Luke I had once volunteered there.

"When were you there?" he asked.

"My junior and senior years in nursing school. Have you ever been there?"

"I volunteered there this past summer," he laughed. *He must have started a few months after I left, just after the arrests!*

We went from an ice-skating date to a roller-skating date, after I'd purchased two pairs of roller skates at Goodwill. We met at the entrance to the tunnel shortly after 5 a.m. on a March morning. It was two hours before shift change, too early for the food carts, and too early for the transporters to be taking patients to the operating room or to X-ray. We figured we'd have about an hour of uninterrupted skating.

Before the sun rose, we roller-skated on every inch of County's labyrinth of musty tunnels. We whizzed past the morgue, past the OR elevators, past the boiler room, and past the Pediatric Building, laughing and shrieking only when we collided with the dirty old mattresses lined up against the walls. Surely we were the first in history to roller-skate in County's tunnels!

Knowing the sun was rising on the old hospital above, we quickly skated back toward Karl Meyer Hall. Directly ahead in the tunnel, also headed toward Karl Meyer Hall, was a bald man in a gray lab coat. Rather than crash into a wall to avoid him, we sped past him.

"Did you know who he was?" I asked Luke later, breathlessly, at the entrance of the tunnel, where we both hastily removed our skates.

"I think he was my attending physician," he laughed. "But I think we were going too fast for him to recognize me. And of course, I'll deny everything." Nobody would have ever believed the attending's story anyhow. They'd think he was hallucinating.

After putting on my shoes, I snuck out the back door of Karl Meyer Hall, and changed into my work clothes in the nurse's residence. It was fun having a boyfriend.

One Saturday evening, we went to dinner and a play. It was a political play. The setting was Nazi-occupied France, and the main character was a member of the French Resistance. He was married with children, but when he was called upon to do a dangerous mission, even though his wife begged him not to go, he went anyhow. In the end he died for 'the cause.'

Afterwards, in a local bar, Luke and I discussed the play. I thought the man should have put his family first, as that was how I was raised to believe.

Luke disagreed. "His wife and family can survive without him. But he had a destiny, a higher calling. He couldn't turn his back on his place in history." I'd never met anyone who thought of life as a destiny, or a place in history. But soon, Luke would have his place in history.

Weeks passed between dates due to conflicts between my work schedule and his on-call schedule. We went out when we could—a dinner in Chinatown followed by a late afternoon walk in Lincoln Park a few Sundays later.

We both had vacations coming up, and it didn't bode well for our budding relationship. Luke was taking a month off in May, to travel with friends in Central America. And I was taking a month off in June. I had planned the trip with my cousin Dennis back in October, before I'd met Luke. We already had our tickets and Eurail passes. *I wouldn't see Luke for two months.*

"Where will you be going in Europe?" Luke asked, shortly before he left.

"We're spending a week in Cambridge, England. We'll be staying with an English doctor and his wife. He spent last summer at County and they rented the apartment above mine. Then we're going to Ireland to stay with Matt's relatives, on the west coast, near Galway. Then we're driving up to Belfast. From there, we're going to Scandinavia, then Germany and Italy."

"Northern Ireland's a war zone right now," he warned. There had been numerous terrorist attacks in the past few months, both in England and Northern Ireland.

"That makes it more exciting," I replied. In some ways I still wanted to be a journalist. Although I really had been looking forward to my trip to Europe, I felt both our vacations came at inopportune times. Two months apart was a long time. He would be a resident with new responsibilities by the time I returned, in June.

# ❖ 38 ❖

The month-long trip to Europe was a wonderful odyssey despite the fact that both England and Ireland were on high terrorist alerts. Several government buildings had been recently bombed and anti-Irish sentiments were on everybody's lips. Our English hosts couldn't understand why we wanted to visit Ireland—they called the Irish "vermin."

But Ireland was our ancestral homeland, and we had to see it. Southern Ireland was hauntingly beautiful, but depressing. So many stone fences around small plots of land with no visible homes, and no source of sustenance on that rocky land. The entire southern part of the country was a vivid reminder of the Great Famine of the 1850's, the decade my ancestors fled. How had my ancestors survived on that harsh, arid, stony terrain? *Why did anyone remain?* I wondered.

Northern Ireland reminded me of Wisconsin—dark, fertile earth. Productive farmland. Dairy farms. We visited Londonderry, a town under frequent attack. We had to park our car in a field on the outskirts of town. I couldn't understand a word anybody said, so thick were their accents.

Our final destination in Ireland was Belfast. The rental car office in downtown Belfast had been bombed, so we had to drive through dreary Belfast to drop the car off at the airport. We could see where sides of hotels had been ripped apart from bombs. Cars couldn't park on streets, for fear bombs would be left in them.

We were greatly relieved to get on the ferry to Scandinavia, where we spent the next three weeks exploring every offbeat town along the Eurail. We toured the fjords in Norway, took the train north of the Arctic Circle, repeatedly toured beer breweries for the free beer in Copenhagen, listened to free music every night in Tivoli Garden, and went past Check Point Charlie into East Berlin. I was a weary traveler by the time I returned to Cook County Hospital on June 5. I wanted to return and continue where we left off.

On July 1, at hospitals throughout the country, a new group of interns arrive, fresh out of medical school. For that reason, July is usually considered the scariest month for nurses and residents in research hospitals, for, depending on where they trained, many of the interns had never drawn blood, started an IV, performed a spinal tap, cardiac defibrillation or CPR, inserted a urinary catheter, given medication to reverse a drug overdose, inserted a naso-gastric tube, or done an EKG, all of which were routinely done by the interns on Ward 35.

My co-workers told me the first week in July had been a terror, that the new group of interns was greener than usual.

"One even tried to insert the IV with the needle going in the wrong direction!" recalled Mrs. Newberry, one of the more outspoken and funny nurses on the floor. "How he managed to get through medical school is beyond me. He must have trained in Pago Pago! And another one put the foley catheter into the woman's vagina instead of her urethra. Blew the balloon up and then thought she was in renal failure because no urine was coming out! We're on high terror alert here."

We nurses had to be more diligent than usual in June. Most interns and med students were encouraged by their residents, ahead of time, to defer to the nurses if they weren't sure of what to do. Some of us gave the interns gentle suggestions and reminders. Instead of asking "What type of IV fluid would you like me to hang?" we'd say, "Here's the D5W IV solution." If the medication ordered seemed inappropriate, we'd say, "Are you sure you want to give that much? In these cases we usually give this dosage." Or "Hyperstat is the drug we usually give in this situation." And if they seemed unsure about a procedure they were performing, we'd ask questions such as, "You *are* going to check to make sure the tube is in the stomach and not the lungs before you inject that liquid, aren't you?"

If the new interns did their medical school training at a hospital that valued and respected nurses, everything went smoothly. If they fought us, ignored us or treated us arrogantly, it was a different story. We could all count on Ms. Newberry to set them straight.

"Sweetheart, I don't care what you wrote on the chart. I ain't givin' *that* dosage of *that* medication. If that patient ain't dead yet, he sure as hell will be when *you* get done with him!" County nurses were the backbone of the hospital, and very few County-trained doctors would disagree.

## ❖ 39 ❖

I rarely saw Luke after I'd returned to work. While I was happily 'touring the continent,' Luke had been elected a leader of the fledgling House Staff Association. The few times I saw him on Ward 35, he unapologetically explained that the House Staff organization, a fairly new union for interns and residents nationwide, consumed *all* of his free time. They were in negotiations with the Governing Commission, he said.

"What is your union trying to accomplish?" I asked. Speaking to him on Ward 35, between examining patients, was now the only time we had together. These conversations were professional, with no hint that we had roller-skated in the tunnel or ice-skated in the park just months ago.

One of their main goals, he said, was to have more input as to how the hospital was managed. He said the negotiating committee, made up of nine members, had drawn up a list of grievances to submit to the Health and Hospitals Governing Commission.

"What kind of grievances?" I asked. The hospital seemed in much better shape than it had been in 1971, when I first started. At least there were doctors.

"Let's start with salary and working conditions," he said. "At County, interns made $11,000 a year. If you figure they work 100 hours a week, on average, that's $1.50 an hour."

"But isn't that the way it is for interns everywhere?" I asked, playing the devil's advocate. "You work like a slave now, but reap the rewards later?"

"I shouldn't have started with the money," he said, "because that's not our major gripe. Primarily, we want to improve patient care. And when interns are up 36 straight hours every third day, and work 100 hours a week, they become careless, and make the wrong decisions. And that's bad for the patients."

I agreed. I didn't know how interns managed to function under intense pressure on the wards all day after being on call every third night. But they did. Internship was the time-honored yearlong initiation ritual for all doctors. But at County, that ritual was even worse in that the interns had to do tasks that support staff did in other hospitals, such as draw blood, do EKGs, and transport patients and lab work all over the place. There didn't seem to be an alternative short of hiring more interns or technicians.

"There's more," he went on, "lots more. This hospital is lacking the basics that other hospitals wouldn't dare be without. Every floor should have a crash cart with defibrillator paddles for emergencies. Right now, you have to search all over the hospital to find one when you need it, and hope it's well-stocked." I agreed with that. Even if you found a crash cart, you often couldn't find a three-prong outlet to plug into!

"Second, the lab should be open 24 hours a day," he continued, "It's absurd that the lab closes at 9 p.m. We can't get STAT results at night or on weekends, even for emergencies, in the busiest hospital in the country!"

"Next," he said, "we need Spanish translators available 24 hours a day. More than half the maternity patients speak Spanish, and there's nobody to translate." I hadn't realized there were that many Spanish patients in OB.

"When I volunteered at the clinic," I told him, "most women said they went to the U of I."

"That's because they have translators over there," he replied, "but this is the County Hospital, and we should be able to serve everyone who comes through these doors," he said.

"And finally," he said, "we need more transporters. Patients wait for hours to go to X-ray, and then wait for hours to get back to their ward. Their IVs go dry, they miss meals and medications, and there's no one to monitor their vital signs."

"Maybe we need *different* transporters, not *more*," I suggested. The transporter's union was a strong one, and the bad ones never seemed to get fired. I often saw transporters hanging in groups behind The Greeks. There was no accountability.

"That's not the point," he said. "There are staff shortages everywhere in this hospital, and you know it as well as anyone. Did you know the Governing Commission has put a freeze on hiring nurses, as of last week?"

I didn't know, but nothing surprised me anymore. Since 1971 there were at least five major threats to close the hospital and numerous layoffs.

"You should see the amount of money budgeted for administrators," he said. "It's obscene. You can't tell me there's money for administrators but not for nurses and basic supplies."

"I suppose I'm used to staff shortages, and making do with what we have," I answered.

"But you shouldn't be! There's no reason it has to be this way. Changes can, and should be made. And since we, the doctors and nurses, are the primary caregivers, it's up to us to point out the deficiencies in the system and demand a response."

I told him how all the doctors had just walked out in 1971 and 1972. They had the same grievances, but when they spoke out, and protested with their ‘heal-in,’ they were fired.

“You weren’t here then,” I said, “but 200 of them left for other hospitals. They gave up the struggle.” And I reminded him that the nurses had gone on strike in 1972 for similar reasons, yet little had changed. Many of the nurses at the bargaining table, including the ones from Ward 35, had also left out of frustration. “It doesn’t take long before dedicated workers burn out---or get cooked.”

“The House Staff Association is in this for the long haul,” he said. His eyes no longer twinkled, and his easy smile wasn’t forthcoming. “We’re committed to improving patient care and public health in this city, and we’re going to make ourselves heard. We’re not asking for much. But what we’re asking for can make a huge difference in the quality of patient care offered at County and at other public health institutions in this country. And we’re prepared to fight.”

He was so serious—a modern day St. Luke. So committed. So focused. So idealistic. Uniting the house staff to reform Cook County Hospital, I sensed, would be a more than full time job for Luke and the other house staff officers. My desire to have a boyfriend would have to take a back seat to the drama about to unfold at County Hospital.

## ❖ 40 ❖

The nursing hiring freeze Luke had mentioned had a direct impact on me. Although my plans to resign in September and join the National Park Service had evaporated, I still planned on leaving County to pursue other interests. One was to learn Spanish. There were too many people I couldn't communicate with as a nurse, and wasn't communicating half the battle in health care? I had been taking evening courses at a community college, but I wasn't progressing fast enough. I applied to CIDOC, a school in Cuernavaca, Mexico that taught Spanish by immersion. I planned to attend for three months.

And finally, as a result of my travels around the U.S. and through Europe, I had developed an interest in history. After learning Spanish in Mexico, I decided to work at the University of Illinois Hospital, which would pay for my college courses and provide more opportunities to practice my Spanish on a daily basis.

All these plans were all put on-hold when I was abruptly transferred to Ward 45 in August to fill in for a nurse on maternity leave. The head nurse was on an educational leave, getting her Masters degree. I learned the ward only had two LPNs and a nurse's aide to care for forty patients! Fortunately, one of the LPNs was certified to give medications.

"You're going to be the *only* RN on a ward with forty patients?!"

asked Elsie, who was now my housemate. I no longer lived in the basement apartment, but had moved upstairs. (In July, the widow Anna had moved back to Norway. My father paid her for her half of the house, painted the walls, and redid the floors and kitchen. Elsie, who worked in Pediatrics, moved in with me.)

I accepted the transfer, but not before telling the head nurse that I'd be resigning in mid-January, so they would have to find a replacement by then. "Not to worry," she said. "We'll both be back by then. And the hiring freeze should be over by then."

Ward 45 was as I'd remembered it as a student clerk with Mrs. Anderson— "twenty mens" on the north wing; "twenty womens" on the south wing. Each wing had a nurse's station for mixing IV fluids, preparing medications and writing notes in the charts. Then, all medications came in bulk jars or bottles. Nurses measured out all dosages and drew up liquid medications such as potassium, insulin and heparin from small glass bottles, all of which looked alike if you didn't read the labels carefully.

The two LPNs worked on one wing, and the nurse's aide and I worked the other. Ward 45 was as great a challenge as any I'd had at County. Those five months could have been a nightmare had the nurse's aide been one who belligerently questioned assignments and complained about being overworked. But I worked alongside sixty-year old Bessie Green, who taught me by example the rhythm of day-to-day patient care. That rhythm included lots of common sense, humor and love. If Mrs. Green had been born in a different time, she'd have been an exceptional RN. But she'd spent most of her life raising her siblings, her own children and her grandchildren.

"There's only two of us and twenty of them so there's no sense making assignments," she told me. "You'll be busy enough with all the IVs and medicines and doctors orders. I'll take care of the rest."

She gave the baths, took routine vital signs, set everybody up for meals, emptied bedpans and made beds. I suctioned lungs, gave medications, changed dressings on bedsores, hung IV fluids, checked cardiac monitors, took vital signs, did patient teaching, conducted range of motion exercises and responded when anyone yelled on the open ward.

"Has it always been like this up here?" I asked her. It seemed like we were running a marathon every day, and I didn't know how anyone could keep up that pace for any period of time. With the amount of work we did every day, I would not have blamed Mrs. Green if she moaned and complained. But she never did.

We worked our tails off, rarely took lunch breaks, and it wasn't long before my weight was down to 100 pounds. Ms. Green said she never had remembered it being this busy, but in the past, she said, there were usually three or four nurses on each floor. They hadn't replaced the nurses who had left, she said.

Mrs. Green helped pace me and keep me from becoming overwhelmed with all the responsibilities of the floor. She was wise beyond words, an earth mother, and so typical of the many older black women I cared for, and came to have great respect for, at Cook County Hospital.

Why wasn't she burned out, I wondered, like many of the other aides I had observed in the hospital. She told me that her faith and idealism kept her going. She said she knew that every act of kindness and care was appreciated at Cook County Hospital. She shared that many of her extended family members had been well cared for at the County, and that it was the kindness and medical expertise of nurses and aides that had helped them overcome their illnesses. She hoped that if she ever became ill, that she would be treated with the same care that she showed others.

On Ward 45, where we were so overworked and understaffed,

the open ward system worked to our advantage because we had twenty extra pairs of eyes monitoring the condition of every patient. If someone became short of breath, needed suctioning, was experiencing pain, or needed the bedpan, the other patients would tell us immediately. The patients knew the routine, they knew who were the sickest patients and they knew our limits. And if someone yelled, you could clearly hear him or her.

If Mrs. Green and I were busy behind curtains with a difficult patient, and the food trays had arrived on the ward, the ambulatory patients helped pass out the trays, and rolled up the heads of beds for bedridden patients. It was the same whether we worked on the men's end or the women's end. It felt like a big family, where everybody helped in whatever way they could with 'the chores.' Working with the same patients every day, I got to know their stories. I was a nurse first, but I longed to take the time to take out my pen and notebook and write down their stories.

But there wasn't even enough time to write nurse's notes in the chart. "Up and about today" usually meant "Feeling well enough to help the other patients today."

Besides working alongside a good-natured aide, I had great interns on Ward 45. All four were bright, idealistic, compassionate, down to earth, and funny. They could just as easily have been Chicago cops, priests, bartenders or garment salesmen on Maxwell Street, with names like Kowalski, Kearny, McGinniss, and Waxler.

Like Luke, the interns and residents on Ward 45 were outraged at the lack of equipment, and how short-staffed we were. All were active in the House Staff Association. Since I rarely saw Luke, they kept me up to date on the progress, or lack of progress, being made in the talks with the Governing Commission and the doctor's demands for reform.

In mid-October, they told me the doctors were planning to go on strike. If they did, it would only be the second physicians strike in U.S. history. Sure enough, on October 27, 1975, over 400 County doctors did go on strike. The doctors passed out informational flyers to clinic patients, asking them to honor the strike and to not come to the County unless it was an emergency. They picketed in three places—in front of the hospital, at the Emergency Room entrance, and in front of Karl Meyer Hall. The attending physicians, who did not take a stand on the strike, covered for them.

The Governing Commission had threatened to deport every foreign doctor who went on strike, regardless of how many years they'd already served. These doctors, especially the third and fourth-year surgical residents, had a lot to lose by going on strike. Yet most of them signed on, and it was quite a sight the day hundreds of medical and surgical interns and residents, American and foreign-born, marched downtown, united, waving their placards, having their date with history.

Every day during the strike I'd gaze out the windows on Ward 45, where I'd see a sea of white coats surrounding Luke and his fellow leaders of the strike outside Karl Meyer Hall. Many of them had long hair and beards. The scene looked like a modern-day Sermon on the Mount.

Nurses from now empty wards joined the doctors on the picket line. I would have too, but I didn't even have time to eat my lunch, let alone leave the floor to picket. Instead, I watched their rallies and interviews on the evening news and read the editorials, at first scathing, then gradually turning sympathetic, in the daily newspapers.

During the doctor's strike, the hospital census fell to around 650 patients (from the usual 1500). On Ward 45, the census remained full.

While other floors were being emptied of patients, Ward 45 was busier than ever and more resembled an Intensive Care unit than a general medicine ward, especially the two-week period when we had two women patients on ventilators. Both had been terminally ill nursing home patients with DNR (Do Not Resuscitate) orders. The night nurse, however, couldn't handle the actual moment of death and called a code when they had stopped breathing. The attending doctors on call, not knowing of the DNR orders, put them on life support systems.

When the day shift reported to duty, we were all dismayed to see that the lives of these long-suffering, terminally ill patients had been prolonged. It was on Ward 45 that I first developed strong feelings about the medical profession's misguided attempts to save every life.

*Why couldn't the medical profession accept death as a natural life passage that should be free from invasive medical procedures?* Instead, these poor souls had to spend their last days on a ventilator, crying out when painful blood gases were drawn and suction catheters were thrust down their lungs several times a day to remove the pooled secretions.

The attending physicians, who had taken over patient care during the strike, were dismayed when they saw how busy Ward 45 was in the middle of the strike. "It looks like Death Row up here!" said one. "Can't we discharge some of these patients?" asked another. After reviewing their charts, all agreed none were ready to go home.

The doctor's strike lasted eighteen days. A contract was negotiated that granted many of their demands, including a slight salary increase, an on-call schedule every four days instead of three, the hiring of more technicians, Spanish translators in admitting areas, training for nurses to do EKGs, draw blood and start IVs, and most importantly, a voice in how the hospital would be managed. One thing they didn't get was faster X-ray and lab service.

After the strike, the seven leaders, including Luke, were sent to Cook County Jail for contempt of court.

"This is a victory for our members and for the patients who use this hospital," said Luke, who, along with his fellow officers, had become media darlings and heroes among their fellow physicians. Their pictures frequently made the front pages of the newspapers, and they were frequently quoted in both local and national newspapers.

"They seem to think they're the saviors of the world," said Dr. James Haughton, contemptuously, after the strike.

Terming the house staff 'the youngest and least experienced group of doctors at the hospital,' Haughton said, despite the contract, he would not permit them to 'dictate' to the commission on matters of patient services.

The strike had both short and long-term implications. It cost the hospital $80,000 a day in lost revenue. But the settlement set a precedent by surrendering a share of authority held by hospital management to the doctors who manned the wards. Interns and residents across the country followed the strike with intense interest for what had really been negotiated was *who* would run teaching hospitals in the future. And at County Hospital, many of those doctors who led the strike *would be* running the hospital in the future.

## ❖ 41 ❖

The strike ended in early November. But working conditions on Ward 45 remained essentially the same—unbelievably busy. December was a record cold month, and my car refused to start the entire month. So every morning was a mass transit ordeal. Up at 5 a.m. Waiting on the dark corner for the bus at 5:30. Shivering on the frigid, windy El platform in a dangerous neighborhood at 6:15. Getting zipped into the crowded train at 6:20. Trudging the three blocks to work at 6:45. I never had time for breakfast and I was freezing, hungry and exhausted by the time I got to work.

It irritated me to hear that other wards were practically empty, yet I received no nursing relief. Every morning, after checking the status of all the patients, I'd called in 'the color code' and the attendance to the nursing supervisor's office, as required. Every day, I'd tell the voice at the other end, "Our ward is full. We have four staff members, ten reds (critical patients), 20 blues (semi-critical), and ten yellows (stable patients)."

"Thank you," said the voice at the other end.

"What's the point of my calling in these colors every day?" I asked Mrs. Green. "If the purpose is to help the supervisors determine if you need additional help, it sure doesn't seem to be working. I could tell the voice at the other end that I have twenty reds, and she'd probably just record it and forget about it. I haven't seen one supervisor since I've been up here."

The stress was getting to all of us. The doctors complained to me that the two LPNs couldn't keep up with all the work and were starting to make mistakes. "I tell the supervisor every day how busy it is," I insisted, "but she never comes by to even see what I'm talking about. She just tells me it's busy everywhere. Maybe if you guys spoke with her, we'd get some extra help."

A few days later, on my day off, an elderly stroke victim died suddenly while eating lunch in his geriatric chair. Mr. Porter had been one of my favorite patients when I worked on the male wing.

He was a retired train porter, had ten children, 32 grandchildren, and he wasn't sure how many great-grandchildren. He had full retirement benefits, but his family brought him to the County—"our hospital." He told me, as best as he could because his speech was slurred, about his trips around the U.S. on the trains. Forty-four years on the trains. He was slowly improving, regaining use of his right side each day. We estimated he'd be ready to go home within a week.

Since Mr. Porter was a big man, the more well male patients helped me transfer him from his bed to his geriatric chair. Everybody enjoyed listening to Mr. Porter's stories about working on the trains during the Jim Crow period of government-sanctioned segregation. The younger patients couldn't believe he wasn't allowed to eat in the same restaurants as his white co-workers. I had traveled with my family to the south in the sixties, and remembered the gas station bathrooms and water fountains that said 'Whites Only.'

I was off the day he died but the other patients told me his head just dropped into his lunch tray. Several patients ran over to him and couldn't get him to respond. That was the one day the supervisor did come to the floor. She questioned whether the medication LPN might have given insulin instead of heparin, a blood thinner. Both were clear fluids that came in small vials. She wrote up an incident report.

At County, there were so many potential problems with giving medications. We received large bottles of the most common pills, and we often had to break the pills into two or four pieces to get the prescribed dose. Pharmacists were never on the wards. Everything had to be mathematically calculated by the nurse, including IV fluids containing medication. In most hospitals and nursing homes, one nurse is assigned to medications only, to prevent distractions. On Ward 45, the medication nurse did everything else as well.

By the time the head nurse returned from her educational leave, I was cooked, and resigned from County, as planned. The staff gave me an emotional send-off on that sub-zero January day. We were a functional family in a dysfunctional place.

Shortly after I punched the clock for the final time, I had to attend an 'exit interview' in the supervisor's office in the basement. I assumed this would be the time they would ask me about my experience working on Ward 45, why I was leaving, and if I had any suggestions for improvement. I was ready to share my thoughts.

The supervisor wasn't there, so my exit view was handled by a clerk. She said all I had to do was sign the form. "It's a good evaluation," she said. "Just sign it."

I noticed my "vital statistics" were typed on the cover sheet: name, age, race, and the ward I worked on. My race was listed as Black.

"Who evaluated me?" I asked, after she handed me the stapled pages.

"The nursing supervisor," she said, and pointed to the signature at the bottom of the first page. It was a name unknown to me.

"I've never met this person," I said. "She's never been to my floor and she's never watched me work." *And obviously she hadn't met me.*

"If she's never been to your floor, that means you've been a good nurse and never got in trouble. It's a good evaluation. Go on. Just sign it." She handed the form back to me. I passed it back to her, unopened. I told her about my past six months on Ward 45 and how no help was ever forthcoming from the supervisor's office.

"I can't sign it," I said.

A blizzard had begun outside. I headed for the subway in my ankle-length down parka, my head covered with a wool cap and scarf. I passed the Nurse's Residence, Karl Meyer Hall, the empty cans of cat food in the alley, Fantus Clinic, the Main Hospital and The Greeks Restaurant. The wind whipped at me as I passed the statue of Louis Pasteur, and I wrapped my scarf more tightly around my neck. After working only seventeen months as an RN, *I was leaving County* and the finality was harder than I ever imagined!

## ❖ 42 ❖

After resigning, I traveled for two months. I was supposed to spend two weeks with a cousin who was a ski instructor in Aspen. But on the first day, he took me on a ski lift to the top of a mountain, and then skiied away. It was my first introduction to icy moguls, and after flying over the first, I crashed into the next one head first and suffered a concussion. Dazed, confused and exhausted from crawling down the mountain, I finally met up with my cousin at the ski lodge eight hours later. Instead of two weeks, I only spent a few unhappy days in Aspen. I was in a fog from both the concussion and depression over leaving County.

After leaving Aspen, I took a bus up to Idaho Falls, where I met up with another cousin who had just finished a grueling year of nuclear submarine training. Like me, he needed some R & R, so we traveled all over the west coast and southwest.

When I returned to Chicago, I signed on with a Nursing Registry for three months at Wesley Passavant Hospital, located between Michigan Avenue and Lake Shore Drive. Per diem nursing was a new concept in hospitals, and only a few hospitals participated. I hoped to save enough money to spend the summer in Mexico learning Spanish.

The hospital was affiliated with Northwestern Medical School, and, like County, had a three-year diploma school for nurses. The only other hospital I had worked in, besides County, was the University of Illinois Hospital, a state hospital. Wesley-Passavant was the first private one I'd ever worked in, and during the months I spent there, I was assigned to almost every floor in the place.

Unlike County Hospital, where we were no longer required to wear our nursing caps, we were expected to wear them at Wesley-Passavant. Older nurses and even doctors who recognized my cap often acknowledged me with a smile.

"You trained at County?" they'd ask. The cap was a badge of honor and I was treated with respect by nurses and doctors alike. What we'd been told in school was true--County-trained nurses had a reputation to live up to. The doctors who recognized it would often share an "unbelievable" story or two about the week or month they spent there.

Per diem nursing was similar to nursing school in that you had to become acquainted with new staff, new patients, new routines and new procedures every day. I was always assigned challenging patients. One day I'd be on the Urology floor, working with catheters all day, and the next, I'd be assigned to the ENT (Ear, Nose and Throat) floor, working with traches all day. I was often assigned to the VIP floor, taking care of Chicago dignitaries, clergy, publishers, business leaders and politicians.

At Wesley-Passavant, I also noticed that the attending physicians made all the medical decisions. Interns just carried out orders from the residents and attending physicians, whereas at County, the interns made all the decisions and did all the work. At County, attending doctors, like nursing supervisors, had been phantom figures.

It didn't escape my notice that the nursing supervisors at Wesley-Passavant were actively involved in patient care and assessment. They sat through reports, they worked on care plans, they participated in doctor's rounds and planned medical strategy with the doctors, they knew every patient on the floor, and they pitched in when the going got rough. I had a discussion about this with a nursing supervisor over lunch one day. I told the supervisor how surprised I was at their level of involvement in patient care.

I told her that in the year and a half I had worked at County I had rarely seen a supervisor, let alone worked alongside one at the bedside. Then again, I'd rarely seen an attending physician either.

She expressed surprise, but said, "Everybody knows that County Hospital is a challenging place to work. I'm not sure I have what it takes to work there, so I'm in no position to judge anyone else."

Nursing was different in a private hospital. I appreciated the fact that the hospital was well-staffed, so I had fewer patients to take care of. But the relationships between the doctors and nurses was an uneasy one. There was a clear hierarchy and I sensed doctors often didn't want nurse's input. It wasn't the collaborative effort I had found all over County, where doctors routinely asked nurses for advice and took it. As dysfunctional as County was, nurses were valued for their intelligence and experience. They were a vital part of the medical team. You'd often hear residents tell new interns, "Listen to the nurses."

When I was a student nurse, I'd often observe nurses teaching procedures to interns. Perhaps that's why I enjoyed nursing at County--I never felt subserviant to anyone. In fact, I felt extremely appreciated there, by patients, relatives, staff members *and doctors.* In the private hospital, I was seeing the nursing profession in another light. I knew I could never work long-term in an environment where nurses were treated as second-class citizens by anyone! I'd only been a nurse for a year, but I knew a hospital was only as good as its nurses. If this condescending attitude was typical for private hospitals, they wouldn't attract the best nurses. They certainly wouldn't stay!

## ❖ 43 ❖

In June, I boarded the plane for Cuernavaca, Mexico—the vacation spot of kings—to study Spanish all summer. I had a suitcase, a letter of confirmation and about $800 in cash. I made no prior arrangements for living quarters, assuming there would be a dorm on-site. I arrived on a Sunday, took a taxi up a mountain to the school, and was dropped off in front of locked iron gates. There were no people and no housing in sight.

After assuring myself that there were no hidden entrances, and accepting that I'd probably be on my own to find a place to stay, I began walking down the dusty mountain road. Halfway down the mountain, I came across a group of Mexican laborers having lunch alongside their pickup truck.

"Donde esta un hotel?" I asked. "Yo soy student at CIDOC." (Where is a hotel? I'm a student at CIDOC.)

They smiled and started answering in Spanish. When they realized I couldn't understand a word they were saying, one pointed down the hill. Then another suggested, using sign language, that I hop in the back of the truck and they would take me there.

When you are exhausted and helpless in a foreign country, and barely speak the language, you are far more trusting, and take more risks than you normally would. I didn't think twice about hopping into the back of the truck with five Mexican laborers. Fortunately, my trusting instinct paid off for within minutes, they dropped me off at a house with a sign in front that said in English "Rooms to Rent."

Ten minutes later, I became a boarder in a large modern house. For $5 a day, I had a room, two meals a day, laundry service and transportation to school.

I later learned twenty-five people lived in the house--seven students from my school and two families totalling eighteen people—six adults and twelve children who shared four bedrooms. One mother washed clothes by hand all day; the other cooked in the kitchen all day. The grandmother plucked the feathers from chickens all day. The maiden aunt was the only adult female to leave the house, to do the shopping.

One father was a laborer; the other was a taxi driver who dropped us off at school every morning. We took the local bus home.

The school was gorgeous, situated on the side of the mountain overlooking the city below. It was dotted with thatched huts, inside of which students followed the verbal commands of the teacher who never spoke a word of English.

I attended school eight hours a day for two-and-a-half months, learning Spanish by immersion. That meant we weren't allowed to speak English on the school grounds. There were two students per teacher, which resulted in a very intense day.

I was paired with a middle-aged Air Force priest, Padre Bernardo, who, like me, knew very little Spanish. We spent hours each night trying to memorize a lengthy two-way dialogue. First thing in the morning, we had to spit out the dialogue. If either of us couldn't, there was no class that day. We always managed.

At the dinner table in my house, only Spanish was spoken. It was fine for the advanced students who lived there and relished the opportunity to speak Spanish with natives. For me, it was an isolating experience and I felt like an immigrant.

On weekends, Padre Bernardo and I took the Flecha Roja bus to Mexico City and enjoyed speaking English to each other. Every trip was an adventure. On a day trip to Mexico City, I suffered with explosive diarrhea all day. Padre Bernardo had taken me to dinner at Las Mañanitas, one of Cuernavaca's finest restaurants, the night before. It was the only day I was sick in the entire three months. While other tourists spent time climbing the pyramids or sightseeing in the museums, I spent the entire day in the bushes closest to the bus, hoping there would be a plentiful supply of large soft leaves.

Halfway through the summer, my mother visited for a week. On the weekend, we took a bus trip to the silver mining town of Taxco. Enroute, in the rebel state of Guerrero, our bus was pulled over by bandits, and we were lined up against the bus at gunpoint. I insisted to Mom that was not typical when traveling around Mexico, but I don't think she believed me.

I told her we'd go to a quaint town in the desert the next day. Instead of a quaint village, it was a dry, dusty, depressing desert ghetto. Half-naked children ran alongside us in the hot, dusty streets, begging for pesos. *To buy what,* I wondered, taking in the barren surroundings. We were also sickened by the sight of starving mother dogs zigzagging down the streets as if drunk, while their starving puppies ran behind, trying to extract milk from the empty, saggy teats. I imagined this was the type of town the impoverished illegal Mexican immigrants had fled when they came to Chicago.

At the end of the summer, I took the overnight bus to Guatemala, to practice my Spanish in a country recently ravaged by an earthquake. I stayed only two days. After touring the ruins of immense stone churches and observing all the newly homeless families living on the streets, I realized it was time to go home. Time to get back into nursing.

I *did* have a plan and neither Cook County Hospital nor the National Parks were part of it. I wanted to work days, take college courses (anything but nursing) in the evening, and utilize my Spanish. When I returned to Chicago, I accepted a job in the OB-GYNE Clinic at the University of Illinois, as a nurse/translator. They told me 70% of the patients spoke no English and I'd need to do patient interviews in Spanish, assist the doctors with examinations and conduct prenatal and birth control classes in Spanish and English. It was a 9-5 job, no weekends, and the U of I would pay for all my evening college courses. And, it was a great opportunity to practice my Spanish. If I didn't practice, I knew I would forget it all.

Even though it was an interesting and challenging nursing opportunity, I felt sad looking at County every day, right across the street. There was no place quite like the County, and I missed the excitement, the camaraderie and the frenetic energy of the place. But to survive in that high-energy environment, one needed energy. I didn't have the energy for both County and school. County was all-consuming of one's energy. I often wondered how nurses with children managed at home after a day on County's wards.

I was reminiscing out loud about County one day and the Medical Records clerk in the clinic said, "You quit the County?"

My stomach knotted from guilt, as if I'd committed the worst type of sin.

"I can't believe you quit the County," he continued. "That's the best place to work in the city," he said, "good pay, great benefits, and it's easy work."

*Easy work!?* I asked if he was sure he meant *Cook County Hospital.*

"Yeah," he said, grinning, "across the street. I got friends there. They come and go as they please. Nobody checks on nothing there, especially on the night shift! But it's not easy to get a job over there.

That's why I can't believe you left."

"That's what your friends tell you about County?" I gasped. I couldn't believe what I was hearing. It angered me that an outsider had that perception of County and its workers. But what angered me more was the grain of truth to what he was saying. What about the phantom supervisors and the cases of toilet paper that disappeared soon after being stocked on the shelf? And the charts that took days to arrive after a patient was admitted, or worst, lost. Or the transporters that were impossible to find? They were probably his friends.

For every friend like his at County, I was certain there were a hundred or more dedicated and heroic employees. *The Saints.*

"So why *did* you leave?" he asked.

"I was burned out," I told him. "I've never worked so hard in my life as I did there."

That night I wrote a letter to the Director of Nursing at Cook County Hospital. I not only told her how outsiders perceived the hospital but I also shared some of my worst memories with her, including the fact that my nursing supervisor was non-existent.

A week or two later, I received a letter from her. But her response was somewhat like the ones I received a few years later, when I visited the Soviet Union and asked pointed political questions of Soviet tour guides. Like theirs, her response was vague, evasive, and arrogantly 'party-line' in tone.

*Dear Miss Karels...* it began.

*I found your letter most interesting and quite similar to the expressions of other new graduates who find themselves in a state of "reality shock," the discovery that school-acquired values are in conflict with work world values. Often the disparity is so great that the nurse cannot survive in the situation and leaves the place of employ-*

*ment. Kramer describes several phases in reality shock, the most crucial being after the "honeymoon phase" where the new graduate is happy and picks and chooses the parts of the new work experience that are interesting to her. However, when the new graduate begins to daily, and hourly, face conflicting values and ways of doing things for which she lacks the appropriate skills, conflict resolution may be maladaptive and progress toward self discovery and growth is arrested. The conflict is often seen as a struggle between school learned idealism and professionalism, and the neophyte nurse becomes a super efficient bureaucratic technician, or she may blame herself and feel defeated or blame and reject the employing hospital. Since you took the time to express your opinions and share views and information from outside sources with me, I am confident that you were and still are a caring, dedicated young nurse who would again be an asset to our staff and possibly a future change agent, or motivating influence for change. If you decide to rejoin the work force, and again become a part of County's Family, don't hesitate to contact our personnel department, and remember, my door is always open to nurses who need to be heard.*

*Sincerely,*

*The Director of Nursing*

I was *not* a neophyte nurse. If I had been a new grad who trained at a suburban nursing school, I could understand why she might write those words. But I had made it clear in my letter to her that I was a County grad, and that I was very familiar with the workings of the hospital. It was true I was idealistic. Most nurses and doctors at County were. That idealism sustained us. But we were not out of touch with reality. On the contrary, we dealt with the sordid reality of the hospital's bureaucratic inefficiencies every day.

But from the tone of her letter, it seemed as if this unacceptable behavior was grudgingly accepted by the administration, and that the idealists would have to deal with it.

*Was I wrong to have expected a phone call suggesting a face-to-face meeting to discuss my letter?* Didn't she care that these things were happening under her watch?

But months later, I learned she *was* on top of things. I ran into a friend from Ward 35 and asked how things were going back there. She told me there was a shake-up, and that some nursing supervisors had been fired.

"Apparently," she began, "a supervisor was moonlighting at a nursing home in the evenings to make extra money. Then she was needed to work days there, and she called in sick to County. When it got to be more than a day here or there, she asked other supervisors at County to cover for her. It became a chronic situation."

*That must have been my phantom supervisor!*

"There was an on-going investigation for several months. She was fired shortly after you left."

So the Director of Nursing knew that all I had written about was true, but wouldn't acknowledge it in her letter to me! Why couldn't she have just written me, "I am so sorry you didn't get the help you needed, when you needed it. We have fired the supervisor in question and the staffing situation has been remedied."

My faith in the place was somewhat restored. Now there were only a million other problems to resolve, including vanishing toilet paper and linens.

*The wheels of change turned slowly at County, but at least they turned.*

# Epilogue

I never returned to work full-time at Cook County Hospital. Instead, I worked across the street for eight years--at the University of Illinois Hospital. I worked for a year in the OB-GYNE Clinic, later on the oncology floor, and finally in the Emergency Room. My Spanish came in handy everywhere I worked. One of the great things about nursing was the diversity. Every specialty was so different, offering different challenges and rewards. Lateral moves were frequent within the profession. For someone like me, who had other interests, nursing turned out to be the best career at that time, with all its flexibility.

To address staffing shortages, County started an in-house registry for nurses who only wanted to work per diem. Whenever I missed County, I signed up to work a few weekends. Having an in-house registry greatly improved staffing problems. I worked on the Open Heart Surgery Intensive Care Unit (Ward 76), on the Post-Partum floor, or on the Medical Intensive Care Unit (Ward 15) on occasional nights and weekends.

I went to school continually, but only took courses in which I had great interest. In 1980, I received my degree in American History from the University of Illinois. I volunteered as a tour guide at the Chicago Historical Society during the day and worked in the University of Illinois Emergency Room at night.

My father's office automation business was finally taking off in 1984, and he asked if I would do some writing for him on the side. This part-time avocation eventually became a full-time career. After working as an RN for ten years, I moved to the east coast, just outside of Manhattan, and immersed myself in a new career that, like nursing, had been previously foreign to me. In time I became an expert on office automation and travelled all over the country.

It was fifteen years before I visited County Hospital again, in the summer of 2000. I'd heard the hospital might be torn down and I wanted my teenage daughter Beth to see where I had done my nurse's training. I barely recognized my former haunts.

A multi-level parking lot had replaced the settings of many of my County stories—including Ward 35. Karl Meyer Hall, where the doctors resided, had also been torn down to make way for a new Cook County Hospital, an ultra-modern one with 450 beds. Much of the new hospital had already been completed in the summer of 2000.

The nursing school still stood, but had graduated its last class in 1980. With the closure of the school, the nursing residence became an administrative building. Our rooms became doctor's offices and our classrooms became extensions of the medical library. I visited the third floor, where photos of every graduating class previously lined the walls. The photos were gone--put into storage at the Midwest Center for Nursing across the street at the U of I.

I sought out former classmates and co-workers on my visit, and wasn't surprised to find that many of the idealistic young interns I worked with were now heads of departments or attending physicians.

A few of my classmates worked in the newly remodeled Emergency Room, one that combined Medical Admitting, Trauma, the ER and the Ambulatory Clinic on one floor. From what I saw, County's emergency service department seemed more efficient than ever. In 2000, the main Emergency Room was the busiest in the country, handling over 110,000 patients per year. The Pediatric ER alone treated 45,000 children, and the Trauma Unit had 4500 admissions.

Even the surrounding neighborhood had dramatically changed. Burned out buildings had been torn down or converted into affordable inner city housing. Community gardens had replaced glass-strewn lots. And Little Italy had become fashionably chic even though my favorite family-owned Sicilian restaurant, Mategrano's, was boarded up. The Greeks Restaurant, the only watering hole in the medical center, had burned down and was never rebuilt.

The neighborhood around Benito Juarez Free Clinic had also changed dramatically. Casa Atzlan still had the brightly painted murals, but was now a day care center. The Ponderosa Bar was a wholesale food market. 18th Street had a number of upscale Mexican restaurants geared toward tourists. The neighborhood was becoming gentrified and real estate prices were astronomical, I learned.

On my visit, I learned that County was now the largest treatment center in the midwest for AIDS patients. When I left in 1976, AIDS had not yet been identified.

Dr. H and the Governing Commission had been replaced years ago with the Cook County Bureau of Health Services. In 2000, this bureau provided public health care services to 1.5 million people.

The racial, sexual and social barriers so evident in the seventies had become far less prominent in 2000. On my visit, I saw a large number of female and African-American doctors, many of whom were heads of departments.

In 2000, the hospital census was down greatly from the 1970's, perhaps because, with HMO's, Medicare and laws that kept hospitals from refusing patients because of their color, patients had more options. Many surgical procedures that formerly required an overnight stay could now be done on an out-patient basis due to new technology. New and better drugs reduced the number of admissions for asthma, heart disease and hypertension.

Better patient teaching in the community health clinics reduced the number of diabetic complications. Community clinics affiliated with the County were better-organized and provided more patient teaching and preventive health care services.

I visited again in the spring of 2005, to attend the 75th anniversary of Cook County School of Nursing. The new 450-bed hospital had opened in December 2002. It cost the taxpayers $625 million, twice as much as originally budgeted, and was the largest public works project in the history of Cook County. The new hospital was named after the President of the Cook County Board--John Stroger.

While there, a County grad gave several alumni a tour of the new hospital, the most modern one in the midwest. It was a surreal experience, for the hospital went from the 18th century to the 21st overnight. The hospital was air-conditioned, and all charting and lab results were computerized. The block-long wards had been replaced by private and semi-private rooms with TVs. The labor and delivery rooms were airy, cheerful and private. Beautiful works of art lined the walls and fresh flower arrangements filled the lobby. It was a modern marvel!

The old hospital was boarded up, it's fate still in limbo. It had just been named one of the Ten Most Endangered Historic Buildings in America by the National Trust for Historic Preservation. The County Board had hired a firm to investigate ways to reuse the building. An organization called Preservation Chicago had collected thousands of signatures to preserve the historic landmark--to tell the story of Chicago's mission of providing high-quality public health care for its residents. *When you lose the building, you lose the memory of that struggle, and ultimately, the collective memories of all who passed through its doors, including the nurses.*

Clearly, the new high-tech hospital will contribute much toward the morale of patients and staff. But a successful health care program requires more than modern buildings and the latest technology. It requires intelligent, compassionate, and dedicated caregivers--nurses. We can only hope that those in charge will invest as much in nurses as they did in new technology.

Nationwide, there is a drastic shortage of nurses. I learned about this shortage while trying to find a nursing home for my mother. Almost every one was severely short-staffed. I learned from friends that bedside nursing in even the best hospitals resembles a battlefield. Today the average age of practicing RNs is 45 and that the average age of nursing professors is 55.

Nursing is an extremely rewarding profession for men and women of all ages who are intelligent, caring, dedicated, idealistic and hard working. But even the most dedicated can burn out, as my story has shown, if support systems are not in place, if staffing shortages are not addressed, and if they are not treated with respect by physicians.

When these systems aren't in place, nurses leave. The innumerable skills they developed as nurses--time management, organization, working with diverse groups of people, crisis intervention, customer relations, evaluation and assessment, multi-tasking and teaching, to name a few--make them well-suited for other professions that will value them.

When our nation's leaders discuss the future of healthcare for the 21st century, they must address this acute nursing shortage and what's really behind it. For sooner or later, whether we live in the inner city or country, we will all need to be cared for. If we must be cared for by strangers, we can only hope that are well-trained RNs.

Even though I haven't practiced nursing in over twenty years, I've kept my nursing license active, for I treasure it. As a nurse and nursing student, I'd delivered babies, taken care of infants and children, guided women through their pregnancies, responded to emergencies of all sorts, taught middle-aged people how to get and stay healthy, and watched lives end. Finally I've written about it.

Thinking back, I realize that it was not what I gave, but what I received, that made nursing so meaningful to me. What I received from my patients, at a very young age, was an appreciation of life--a recognition that life is a gift we can treasure, take for granted or destroy with neglect and abuse.

Hopefully my story will encourage others to pursue nursing. It is never too late to become a nurse. The profession needs you; and quite possibly, you might need it.

Forty members of my class graduated on June 28th 1974.
The school seamstresses made white graduation uniforms for each of us with the hemline about four inches higher than our student uniforms.

The Board of Directors of

**Cook County School of Nursing**

Chicago, Illinois

Upon the recommendation of the Faculty have granted to

**Carol J. Karels**

this diploma of Graduate Nurse upon the satisfactory completion of a course of professional study and practice.

In testimony whereof, the proper officers of the Board of Directors and of the School have hereunto subscribed their names and caused the seal of the School to be affixed.

Done at The Cook County School of Nursing, City of Chicago, State of Illinois, this twenty-eighth day of June in the year of Our Lord One Thousand Nine Hundred and Seventy-four

President of the Board of Directors

Executive Director of the Board of Directors

Director of the Division of Education

Director

# To Order More Copies of "Cooked"

*Order online at info@arcaniapress.com*

**or**

**Send a check or money order for**
**$13.99 plus $3.95 shipping and handling to:**

**Arcania Press**
**65 Zabriskie Street**
**Hackensack, NJ 07601**

**Please include your mailing address,**
**e-mail and phone number**

**Please call us for quantity discount rate**
**800-669-1330**